THE EMOTIONAL ENTREPRENEUR

scout sobel

To my sister Mads. Inviting you into the entrepreneurial space has been the biggest honor of my life. What exceeded all expectations of what I believed would come out of working together was the self-awareness, emotional resilience, and personal development commitment that you have made not only to yourself, but to your dreams. Watching you move through discomfort as you hold onto a major vision for your life has made me prouder than you can ever know.

This book is for you. All of my lessons are for you. My healing's teachings are for you. Everything I wish for in people, I see in you.

Whenever you are at a crossroads in life, when the fire seems too big to put out, and the self-doubt creeps in, please remember this: I see you, I believe in you, and I will always hold the highest vision for your life when you momentarily aren't able to. I hope this book brings you back to your soul's course time and time again within the cyclical and emotional phases of life.

I'll see you in a few years, presenting you with an award in front of a sea of people when the world is ready to acknowledge what I see in you: a talented, resilient, emotional entrepreneur.

I love you.

Foreword

by Jessica Zweig, Founder & CEO of The SimplyBe. Agency & Author of Be.

"If it were easy, everyone would do it."

As an entrepreneur, I say this to myself in my darkest moments, of which I have many.

Being an entrepreneur is profoundly, brutally challenging.

Not because of the long hours it demands, the fires only you are equipped to put out, the excruciatingly tough decisions you must make on a daily (sometimes minute-to-minute) basis, the clients you must constantly please, and the never ending pressure to drive revenue in order to feed the livelihoods of, you know, real human beings who work for you.

The journey of entrepreneurship is profoundly, brutally challenging not for any of the above complexities but rather, for one simple reason: it's emotional.

Extremely emotional.

It doesn't matter if you are the CEO of a billion dollar tech company or a sole owner starting her one-woman PR firm, no entrepreneur is safe from the acute, sometimes euphoric, but more often painful, emotional roller coaster called "running your own business."

Over the last decade, entrepreneurship has become the sexy, desirable, and trendy thing to do. We are bombarded with a glorified lifestyle on social media filled with #bossbabe imagery, stylish women in pink pastel offices sipping out of coffee mugs that say things like, "The Dream is Free, The Hustle is Sold Separately," while we gaze googly-eyed at mega-entrepreneurs boasting millions of followers and multi-million dollar exits. (It just looks so fun, right!?) Of course it's easy to idolize the sparkly vision of designing your own day, crafting your beautiful logo, untapped earning potential and not having to answer to anybody.

It's true that, as an entrepreneur, you don't have to answer anybody.

You do, however, have to answer to everybody.

I'm talking about unpleasable clients, toxic staff members, dissatisfied online followers and customers, overly protective lawyers, scrutinizing loan officers and bankers, the often critical media, savvy competitors, tech support when your systems fail, and let's not forget your landlord.

But the one person you have to answer to the most is... you.

More specifically, the imposter who lives inside you who questions daily: "Can I actually do this?" There is a massive shadow side to entrepreneurship and it's filled with self-doubt, fear, shame, uncertainty, loads of anxiety and often depression.

For this reason, the journey of entrepreneurship is also incredibly lonely, and here's why:

No one is talking about how truly emotional being an entrepreneur really is.

Until now.

Scout Sobel's book is more than a book, it's medicine. And Scout is more than just your author, she is your healer.

This is because she learned how to heal herself.

For many of us, going into entrepreneurship activates the experience of depression, anxiety and paralyzing overwhelm. For Scout, becoming an entrepreneur herself saved her from the depths of this darkness. Entrepreneurship became the key vehicle that allowed Scout to finally heal herself from her bipolar disorder and turn her entire life around, proving everyone wrong who doubted her, all while scaling a 6-figure business along the way before the age of 29.

In The Emotional Entrepreneur, Scout takes you deep into the piercing, bullseye experience of what it really feels like to start, build, and scale your own business. Through a series of 25 Lessons, each filled with expert wisdom from real-life experiences, soulful guiding questions and perhaps most sacred of all, Scout's own personal vulnerabilities, you are officially no longer alone on this path of being an entrepreneur.

This book will set you free from the shame, self-limiting beliefs, uncertainty, and loneliness you most likely feel at this moment. It will wipe away the stigmas around mental health and create space for you to get honest with your feelings, all while giving you powerful but practical tools to show up like the brave, brilliant boss you truly are.

I believe in what this book will do for you, and how deeply it will change your life. I believe in how much Scout believes in you. I believe in Scout. That's because she believes in me.

I am blessed to call myself a client of Scout's Agency, which has represented me for almost two years. Earlier this year, when I launched my own book, Scout single-handedly helped me get on over 50 podcasts, which in turn connected me to the biggest thought leaders in the industry, grew my Instagram following by 4000 in less than one month, and helped my book become a #1 best-seller overnight. None of this would have been possible without her.

This book consists of that same care, commitment, compassion, and sheer belief Scout provides for her clients, family, friends and now with you, her readers. The dedication she has to your professional, mental, and emotional success is palpable in these pages.

My wish for you is that with every turn of the page of The Emotional Entrepreneur, you are reminded that your emotions are not your weakness.

They are your superpower.

Contents

My Story

I remember.

I remember my life as a string of countless beads, each representing extreme uncertainty and crippling pain. I remember the milestone moments of my teen and early adult years were those that kept me stagnant or made me regress. I remember the hospitals, the medication, the therapist offices. I remember tears that didn't seem to stop and a beating heart that existed in overdrive.

I also remember finding entrepreneurship—my first milestone that began to weave a different story, created a different string of beads that would adorn my neck and I would one day wear with pride and confidence. I remember the healing and the wisdom I found in cracks of despair. I remember the relief my husband felt once he internally knew I could take care of myself. I remember the trip to Barnes & Noble to see my magazine on the newsstands, the moment the Okay Sis podcast made Apple's top podcast charts, the way I felt when my agency hit a six-figure revenue in its first year, the confidence I felt when I started supporting myself regardless of living with bipolar disorder.

I remember it all, and yet not one of those moments ultimately defines who I am now.

Instead, what defines me now is an amalgamation of my past, present, and future. I had my first depressive episode when I was only fourteen. A cumulative storm created by a breakup, the delivery of my mother's multiple sclerosis diagnosis, and my first two months of high school swirled me into a destructive pattern of self-harm, restricting food, wearing sloppy sweats to school each day, and self-isolating in my room every night to cry and listen to emotionally driven songs. My school quickly found out about the self-harm and notified my parents, who put me in therapy immediately. I resisted therapy and had to visit three or four before my angsty teenage self would actually give the process a chance.

My first therapist spoke about himself mostly, which, as a fifteen-year-old girl who had never experienced therapy and didn't have any friends in therapy, I marked as normal. He had me take a five-hundred-question test to determine the stability of my mental health. I dreaded taking it, filling in the multiple-choice bubbles as if the intricacies of my emotional mind could be encapsulated in a scale of one to five. The results were illuminating, regardless of my skepticism. I ranked on the border of clinical and chronic depression. I remember sitting in his office receiving the news, thinking that some part of my life would be changed, that the trajectory would be different.

But nothing happened. I was not put on medication. The diagnosis was given and then discarded. A lot of what I was feeling was chalked up to teenage hormones. And despite the fact that my depression and anxiety were so crippling that I was often unable to complete homework assignments, not out of cognitive difficulty but out of overwhelming emotional paralysis, I was left alone to visit his office twice a month in hopes that my inability to move through life as gracefully as my peers could be solved within those stingy hours.

I went up and down in high school. I had moments of feeling passionate about life and moments where everything seemed too difficult to handle. I was always the friend who was anxious about sneaking out to go to a party and always voiced my concerns. I never felt invincible. I always predicted the worst.

It wasn't until I went to college, a few short months after my parents announced they were getting divorced, that my mind escalated from depression and anxiety to psychosis and paranoia. I would wake up in the middle of the night, frozen from head to toe with fear that men were in my closet, under my bed, or on my balcony, waiting to come harm and kill me. I would plan escape routes without moving a finger. I would walk home from class and believe there was a man with a gun following me who, at any moment, would open fire on me. Parts of me knew these were illusions and parts of me believed them. My mind was exiting reality and creating its own daunting one just for me.

I was twenty years old when I was diagnosed with bipolar disorder. Back then, the words "mental health," "bipolar disorder," or even "self-care" were not mocked up as aesthetically pleasing quotes on Instagram in hopes of destigmatizing and opening up the conversation. Just 10 short years ago, I felt alone, crazy, and done for.

Freshly dropped out of college, I tried everything from a minimum-wage job as a gelato scooper to interning at C Magazine to taking night classes at UCLA to get back in the game. I quit every single one of those commitments while my family held their breath in hopes that I could follow through. I had panic attacks in fancy restaurants in Paris on our family vacation, and I called in sick from my job with the help of psychiatrist notes. I was put on medication— an endless trial-and-error journey that oftentimes left me physically wrecked or emotionally worse. My parents sat in doctors' offices and listed to talk of my never being able to function in society. I was placed on a 51/50 where I was legally deemed a threat to myself and to society and was strapped to a stretcher and escorted by an ambulance to the inpatient wing. I had suicidal ideation. I heard voices in my head. I developed catatonia; my body became physically paralyzed, and I could not speak for hours on end because my nervous system was so abused from anxiety, it just shut down. I had spurts of hypomania, which I don't often address because they were harmless and quite fun. I entered such states of depression that I took down everyone around me. I entertained the idea of electric shock therapy because no medication was working. I entered into an outpatient program, twice.

These are the events of the past fifteen years of my life, but there is one thing that kept me going, getting me out of bed each day, and painting my life with purpose and passion—and that is entrepreneurship.

My husband was the one to prompt me down a road of healing when he looked at me, just a few months into dating, and said, "I don't care if you are depressed. If you are depressed and hopeful, I can be here with you. If you are depressed and hopeless, I cannot be in this relationship."

After losing so much to my bipolar disorder, I decided I wasn't going to lose him too. I got to work, bought all the self-help and psychology books, started going to support groups, listing things that I was grateful for, and most importantly, infusing hope into my days, regardless of how I felt.

After a year or so of taking my healing into my own hands—where, believe me, panic attacks, depressive episodes, and crying fits still happened on a regular basis—the fruits of that hope visited me one day at a coffee shop when an idea popped into my head. I asked my friend if she wanted to start a magazine with me, and the rest, as they say, is history.

When I found entrepreneurship, I knew I'd found my home. Entrepreneurship and my bipolar disorder had similar patterns: they both cycled through high highs and low lows. I was used to emotional waves, and I was used to cycling between them at a moment's notice. Therefore, I felt as if I could live within entrepreneurship's rollercoaster because its track was highly similar to the one my mind had grown accustomed to.

It also gave me something outside of myself to be dedicated to and passionate about. It allowed me to design my life on exactly my terms—something very important for someone with a mental illness—and it provided me with responsibility and accountability, for if I didn't show up, no one would. I fell in love with its dance, with creating businesses and products and services, with branding, with pivoting, with market research, with the excitement of the sale.

This book is not specifically for the mentally ill, but it is one for those who subscribe to their own mental health and want to be entrepreneurs. I found that entrepreneurship was the biggest personal development game one could play—it will highlight your shadows, your weaknesses, and your deepest insecurities while simultaneously putting your strengths, your vision, and your zone of genius on full display. Navigating the birth, creation, and management of your business, whether that is an Etsy shop, a YouTube channel, a direct-to-consumer product, or a service-based agency, is highly emotional.

With the experience of walking through fire and out the other side, I have been able to implement the emotional lessons my bipolar disorder gifted me and use them to fuel the success of my businesses. Today, the girl who dropped out of college, was hospitalized, and lived in a place of painful uncertainty about the future is now an agency owner, a podcast host, and an author.

Today my entrepreneurial life looks like this (and it has gone through many, many iterations): I run Scout's Agency, which I founded in February of 2019. We specialize in getting women as guests on podcasts and also feature our clients in digital media publications. In the first year, I had accumulated a six-figure revenue. In the second, I doubled that revenue. With no prior experience in public relations, I was able to sign incredible women and female-founded brands to my roster within the first year and a half—like Catt Sadler, Rebecca Minkoff, Bala, Jessica Zweig, Cathy Heller, Damona Hoffman, and Kelley Baker. I placed my clients on top podcasts like Lady Gang and Almost 30 while also getting them press features in magazines like Vogue, Forbes, Harper's Bazaar, ELLE, Women's Health, and O, The Oprah Magazine and digital platforms like Refinery29 and BuzzFeed. I have created a team of amazing women who help me support our incredible female clients and have fun along the way.

I also am the co-host of the Okay Sis podcast with my sister, Mady. We have interviewed women like Trinity Mouzon Wofford, Sivan Ayla, Lauryn Evarts Bosstick, Amanda Stanton, Lauren Elizabeth, Dom Roberts, Kenzie Elizabeth, Zuri Hall, Heather McMahan, Koya Webb, and Orion Carloto. We have created an incredible community, which we call "the sisterhood," of women who are strong, vulnerable, creative, and passionate. Apple listed us in their New & Noteworthy section, and we have been on the top charts in the Society & Culture category. We have worked with advertisers such as Warby Parker, HUM Nutrition, and Thrive Causemetics.

I also am the host of the SCOUT podcast, where I talk openly about mental health, spirituality, and entrepreneurship. After being vocal about living with bipolar disorder on Okay Sis and receiving feedback from our listeners who were filled with inspiration and hope, I knew I had to dedicate a place for content that was centered around healing, strength, and mental health.

And now, I am the author of the book you are currently holding and reading.

All of my entrepreneurial successes came from my superpower—being able to navigate my emotions. This superpower was birthed from the petals of pain I was given through my mental illness. This book is a heartfelt outline of the twenty-five most important lessons my bipolar disorder taught me, lessons that I have implemented in my entrepreneurial life to drive me towards success.

In this book, you will find lessons that will help you manage fear, understand risk, unearth limiting beliefs, and learn how to believe in yourself so that you can wake up each day and build the life you have been dreaming about. It is a book you can read straight through, and it is a book you can work through topic by topic, depending on your emotional needs for the day. Whichever way you read it, I hope that it brings you strength, clarity, and confidence.

As emotional entrepreneurs, we know that our ability to navigate our feelings is what is going to bring our ideas into this world successfully. It is my biggest wish for you and, I hope, my biggest gift with this book—that you wake up each and every day and know in your bones that no matter what life throws at you today, you are ready, willing, and open because you fundamentally believe that you are safe in your emotions and you know that this lifetime is the one where your dreams are destined to become a reality.

If you're not there yet, don't worry. This is the journey I am about to bring you on.

You are about to become The Emotional Entrepreneur.

ENTREPRENEURSHIP
IS JUST A MIRROR
THAT WILL SHOW
YOU WHO YOU ARE
AND WHAT YOU ARE
MADE OF.

Lesson #1:

It's Personal And Emotional

"I never subscribed to the mentality of 'Nothing personal, it's just business.' Because 'just business' implies that my work can be distilled to 'just' numbers or cells on a spreadsheet. For me, business is personal. Because business is built by and for humans. Emotive, needy, and complex humans. When you connect to your audience's humanity, not only are you rewarded financially but personally. So, no. It's not 'just business' for me."

-Mady Maio, co-host of Okay Sis Podcast and co-founder of Camber

_y time I record a podcast, there's a sacred moment after having shared space for forty-five minutes talking about successes, challenges, dreams, and current fixations, that we wind down our interview with a question that eases tension, melts shoulders, and causes hearts to sing. We ask our guest, "If you could brag about one thing in your life, and don't be humble, what would you brag about?"

They usually go silent. Earlier moments of back and forth banter quiets as they sit in utter reflection; moving inward through the stages and milestones of their lives. They take their time; they ponder. And while they pause, we get to witness their sweet surrender to the montage of their life. We get to witness them receiving permission to exhibit pride and to share those moments of their lives that changed the course of their emotional blueprint forever.

Because at Okay Sis Podcast, we don't just celebrate women, we encourage them to celebrate themselves. We get to see the personal behind the business.

The personal is where I thrive, where I get to play and develop, where I get to grow. It is also the place that has historically been negated from the entrepreneurial narrative. We have all heard the phrase, *"It's not personal, it's just business."* And while yes, our worth as human beings living in this ever energetic world does not diminish if someone does not buy our product or enroll in our course or choose us to run their social media, it doesn't mean that building our businesses isn't personal. For me, it's been highly personal from the moment I entered the game and reclaimed my life.

We all know there are resources that teach us to balance our PnL, but what about the part of you that is yearning to learn how to navigate the fear of opening up your own business? The part of you that is afraid of risk but is learning how to deal with it anyway? The part of you that acts outside of the box and needs to learn how to take on responsibility? That part of you that knows that your business is only as strong as your ability to persevere, pivot, and process?

That is the part of you that is yearning for the personal in the giant game of designing your life the exact way it has played out in your dreams over and over and over again.

I learned that business was personal the moment I entered it, because it engaged a complete emotional transformation within. When I finally found entrepreneurship, I was 22, recently diagnosed with bipolar disorder, a college dropout, working part time as a barista, and had been told by psychiatrists and therapists alike that I wasn't going to be able to function in society.

And then an afternoon at the neighborhood coffee shop changed everything. I brought home an indie magazine from my favorite bookstore in Manhattan because the pages of fashion magazines were where I allowed my imagination to run wild. I remember being thirteen and claiming the monthly edition of Teen Vogue when it was delivered to our home, letting my sister know she could only touch it once I had completely devoured each page. The moment I realized what a career was, I declared that I would be an Editor-In-Chief of some sort. So, almost 10 years later, I carried a beautifully bound magazine back from New York to this Newport Beach coffee shop to sip chai lattes with my friend and flip through the avant-garde fashion spreads. And suddenly, as if an inner force was moving through me, I looked up at her and I asked: "Do you want to start a magazine?"

I immediately got to work, as if a flashy needle was threading a large and exciting tapestry on automatic. I experienced a force that was pulling me forward when I was so used to remaining stagnant within my mental illness.

That magazine plummeted me into a whirlwind journey of launch ing a successful Kickstarter campaign, negotiating Barnes & Noble contracts, photographing Halsey for our cover, schlepping magazines across Southern California to distribution warehouses, endless meetings with my graphic designer, and planning a fancy launch party at The Standard in West Hollywood. I was living a scrappy yet glamorous life. More importantly, I had proven to myself that I could follow through and handle something—anything!—within the framework of society. I added it to the list of growing evidence that would prove my doctors wrong.

That magazine was my first baby. Its three-issue creation led to many tears and many stressful days but also to immense fulfillment and joy. I learned what I was capable of, what my thresholds looked like, and that I could build confidence by following through with an idea. It helped me come home to myself: the emotional entrepreneur.

You picked up this book because you have a ferocious cry within that wants a life of purpose. You also know navigating that life will come with many emotional challenges. You will need to learn to feel safe in those emotions because you've probably also heard the phrase, "Entrepreneurship is a roller coaster." That reality is true, yes, but it's up to you whether the roller coaster is fun and thrilling or daunting and distressing. And it starts with identifying your emotional landscape and upping your mental strength—an art I have been studying since I experienced my first depressive episode at the age of fourteen.

My definition of business is that it is an exchange of monetary value that lives within a larger framework: be it an agency, an Etsy shop, or a brick and mortar. My definition of entrepreneurship is that it is a wildly passionate, emotional, and gritty pursuit to live life according to the terms you contracted yourself to live within. It is the pursuit of the soul— your soul. In the spirit of that, we can ditch the PnLs for just one second because at the end of the day, if you learn how to make money and don't know how to enjoy the inner workings of your being, what is the point?

So, yes, pursuing your passion is extremely personal. Because it's your life. At the end of the day, entrepreneurship is just a mirror that will show you who you are and what you are made of. It will show you what it wants you to rise up to and where it knows you can go—if you can place the ego aside for one moment to truly listen.

Let's have that mirror reflect you in complete, majestic, and sometimes messy alignment with your soul.

Let's have it reflect you as the perfectly competent and big-time-dreaming emotional entrepreneur that you are.

The Lesson: Your emotions are your guiding superpowers when it comes to building the business of your dreams.

WHAT TYPE OF PAIN DO YOU WANT TO TAKE ON FOR THE REST OF YOUR LIFE?

Lesson #2:

Get An ROI On Your Pain

"Your soul chose to incarnate in this lifetime to learn, transform, and grow through a series of challenges, and your soul's purpose is to share these lessons to inspire and support others on their journey. If you could teach the whole world one thing that changed your life the most, what would it be?"

-Amber-Lee Lyons, Founder of Chakra Girl Co. and Prism

I have a close friend. She's called Pain. I'll place a bet you've met her too.

I like to define pain as that thick, inevitable emotion we all experience in life. Those moments where your body feels overtaken by an emotion so pungent and heavy that you are unsure if you are ever to feel without it again. It sinks your heart, constricts your chest, increases your heart rate, and convulses your mind.

When painful emotions used to overcome me, I would ask myself: What is pain's purpose? Its crusade? Rationally, I know that pain exists to keep us safe. It is a guardian. Our ancestors relied on pain to keep them alive; it's embedded in our DNA so we don't place ourselves in inherent danger. Biologically it has kept our lineage alive.

However, when I look at the landscape of modern times with the internet, cosmopolitan cities, and social media, I increasingly see that most of us freeze in our comfort zones instead of jumping into the vast unknown, where possibilities can expand and soar. We know that if we step into uncertainty, there is a chance we could experience pain. In a sense, our entire lives are made up of choices to avoid this heavy, uncomfortable emotion. Little decisions that keep us playing small because in the realm of playing small, your chances of injury are much slimmer.

Biologically, our bodies and minds send out signals to keep us safe at all costs. Anxiety visits as a warning that we are entering into unknown territory where pain might exist. But let's be consciously realistic: today, the kind of threat we are talking about is an angry email or an upset customer, not a buffalo stampeding toward us.

(Quick note: this is not to sweep by the real and physical dangers many people live with on a daily basis. For the sake of this book, I am talking about the emotional experience of staying small in a setting where you have the option to play big. I am talking about pain within

the confines of today's society, entrepreneurship, and mental health. There are too many people on this planet who still do not have safety as a right, and I understand that this type of pain we experience is a privilege.)

This is all to say that our minds don't understand the difference between being hunted down by a bear or having a warehouse fuck up our production order, causing a tight cash-flow situation for the future of your business.

So, we are programmed to be alerted when pain might be around the corner, but we are also living in disconnect if we are sinking into the safe bubble we all know as our comfort zone.

There were many days that pain pinned me down and kept my life trajectory quite consistent—low, but consistent. There were days it surprised me and ruined plans, like that time I cancelled a trip to Paris the very last minute because my entire body was pulsating with anxiety. It is the reason I dropped out of college and the reason I didn't take initiative in my healing at an early age. With everything I did, I came to believe that the entire human experience was just too painful.

When you experience endless pain with no growth or forward movement, you are not receiving a very good return on investment. If we have to feel pain, and we will (so let's accept that one real quick), why not have that pain propel us toward growth versus stagnation?

One morning, I was on the phone with a friend, and she was venting to me about how much anxiety she was experiencing at work—so much so that she had to take medication just to get through certain obligations. Her extreme emotional discomfort was painful, leaving her empty, depleted, and sad. She wanted to pivot into a new career or a new job or a new anything but was afraid of meeting the discomfort of that process.

When she talked about her discomfort, I realized I'd had similar debilitating anxiety that day about a client's account with my agency, Scout's Agency, that just wasn't getting the best results. The only difference was that I was building the business of my dreams and creating a life of opportunity that I wanted to be in. In contrast, she wanted to get out of her reality as quickly as possible.

I said to her, "We are both experiencing pain in our careers, but you're not getting an ROI on yours. I am. If you're going to be experiencing moments of discomfort, wouldn't you rather it be propelling you toward fulfillment?"

That simple statement changed her life and mine, and it can change yours too. Take a moment to examine your pain. Is your anxiety coming up because you cannot walk through that office door one more time? Or is your anxiety prevalent because you spent forever preparing a presentation for your dream client and you're waiting for her thoughts? Are you in deep discomfort because your boss doesn't respect time boundaries and you've had to miss date-night for the third time in a row? Or are you consciously deciding to not stop by that party because you have your first webinar launch tomorrow and you want to get a good night's rest, even though your friends keep blowing up your phone with a hint of annoyance?

This is the point where you decide what pain you want to endure. Do you want to live your life through a worn-out and diluted perspective? Or do you want to jump off a cliff and put yourself out there, knowing a big reward is one choice away?

I cannot take all of life's pain away from you, and I wouldn't want to even if I could. If given an option, I would not choose a pain-free life, no matter what the Garden of Eden promised me. Pain is this thing that forms, molds, and inspires us, if we let it. It pumps itself through us when we aren't living out our purpose, and then it asks us how badly we want it when we start doing just that.

It continues to show up as you scale your business, as you succeed, and as you fail. There's always another step to conquer, always a new experience to navigate or gain perspective on. With those new growth opportunities will come discomfort. You must decide if your pain is making you stronger, or if it's keeping you in a state of consistent suffering.

Ask yourself: what is the ROI on my pain?

Pain has visited me in the following experiences as an entrepreneur:

- Feeling the pressure of having an entire business operation on my shoulders
- Being responsible for all of the finances
- Being responsible for the work culture of my company so that my employees are fulfilled and inspired
- Having anxiety over inconsistent income
- Managing never really being "off" the clock
- Knowing that I am the one who handles all crises, regardless of whether or not I created the fire in the first place
- Hiring someone new and feeling the urge to vomit because I am now responsible for someone's full-time salary
- Figuring out how to respond to an angry client who wants to end their contract with me (not on good terms)
- Not being able to take a real vacation where I don't start my days with work
- Navigating the pressure of having no real paid maternity leave when the time comes
- Taking large amounts of monthly retainers from clients and wanting to show up for them in a way that is big and purposeful
- Feeling like a complete fraud
- Coping (again) with the overwhelm of everything being on my shoulders

But the ROI? It's deliciously sweet:

- I get to create my own schedule, giving me complete freedom over my days
- I can travel around the world and work from wherever I desire or choose
- I get to organize my business in a way that best serves the way I process and work
- I get to make creative and executive decisions, thereby influencing the future of my business
- I get to pivot my business in any way I desire if I need a new challenge or want to spruce things up
- I have total creative freedom
- I am in charge of my future and my destiny
- I get to establish my salary and know that it is not fixed
- Every single night, I go to bed proud and fulfilled
- Every single morning, I wake up excited and ready to get to work

I know it's a strange, counterintuitive question to ask: what type of pain do you want to take on for the rest of your life? But it is in that answer that your future will develop and dance. The discomfort you are willing to take on will illuminate your canvas or destroy it before it sees the light of day.

I hope you choose to get a return on investment instead of floating around in suffering purgatory.

Even when I wrote this, I was on vacation with my husband for my birthday, staying in an oceanfront room (we fell asleep to the sounds of waves crashing onto the sand) with mimosas galore. And still, amidst all the relaxation and glamour, I was anxious to my core. A client didn't get back to me the day before, and I had the inkling she was unsatisfied with my work, a reality that comes with the job when you provide a subjective service.

I sipped my coffee the next morning watching the waves, holding my husband's hand, and got to be reminded of my ROI. I reminded myself that this moment of discomfort stemmed from something completely out of my control, that I was ruminating on something that was truly Monday's responsibility. In order to let go of a situation that, quite honestly, I was completely catastrophizing and would, at the end of the day, be no big deal, I had to look out onto the waves and put my ROI into perspective.

I was given this uncomfortable test as a reminder of why I do what I do—not to run from discomfort, but to move through it so I get my return and continue to build and build and build.

Here is a law of emotional entrepreneurship: We don't run from hardship, whether that is an upset client or owning up to a mistake we made while building our dreams and putting things into motion. We face it knowing very well how every little step will propel us forward.

Every little step will bring us a return on our emotional investment.

The Lesson: Make sure everything you do on a daily basis that involves "discomfort" promotes your growth, not stagnation.

FUCK FEAR. ACCEPT DISCOMFORT. ACCOMPLISH COOL THINGS.

Lesson # 3

Fear Is The Silent Killer

"Turn fear into your biggest motivator, change your mind set on the word and its entirety and your whole world will change."

-Lindsey Carter, Founder of Set Active

I am notorious for starting projects. I started a magazine, when I was 22. I was on the founding team of a digital women's media site at the age of 24. I started a blog. I started my own podcast, which then led me to starting the Okay Sis podcast, which then led me to starting the SCOUT podcast. I was the Director of Operations for a tech start-up. I started Scout's Agency, which I currently run, and now I've written this book.

Sometimes, my family gets a little fatigued when I tell them about a project. They most likely count down in their heads until I move on to the next one.

I, however, see things a bit differently. Every new project and new iteration of my career has landed me here. Here is looking pretty magnificent, miraculous, and inspiring—at least to me. Every decision I made, everything I started and stopped, every time I pivoted and stumbled into a different business medium, got me here, writing these words that you are currently reading. The only reason all of these projects and accomplishments happened is that I am pretty damn good at saying fuck off to fear.

Fear drains, envelops, and suffocates. It changes the trajectory of your future. It swallows ideas whole. It paralyzes our purposeful action, and it silently, yet somehow with such rational justification, kills our dreams.

So many times, human beings will not take the first step out of fear of the complete unknown, of failure, of challenging times ahead (and as we chatted about earlier, in an effort to avoid pain). They stay cocooned in their bubbles because those mundane bubbles are better than risking and sacrificing to potentially reach greatness, purpose, or fulfillment, regardless of the fact that life is uncertain, even with the corporate job or marriage contract.

In the face of uncertainty, I believe that we must still act—that it is our duty as beings to act. Here's how I do it.

Whenever I want to start a project or throw myself into something creative, and I feel a hint of resistance, I ask, "Fear, is that you?" If the answer is yes, I know I have to do it anyway. Godspeed to my ear, because I am about to act without its permission, and I am going to make decisions without its vote. I am going to make shit happen with a fervor and a force fear would be afraid of.

If I let fear run my life, my dreams, and my aspirations, I wouldn't have received an email a few weeks ago saying I had been nominated for Forbes 30 Under 30 (which I did not get in the end but celebrating myself for the nomination!). I wouldn't have sipped wine over Zoom with my sister and Kaitlyn Bristowe as a guest on her podcast, *Off The Vine*. I wouldn't have hosted a live event with Cassie and Michelle Randolph for the Okay Sis podcast at The Dream Hollywood Hotel, where we packed the lobby and got to meet some of our most loyal listeners and had the sobering moment of realizing this is all for us? I wouldn't have worked with clients like Catt Sadler, Cathy Heller, Bala, Jessica Zweig, Rebecca Minkoff, and Kelley Baker. I wouldn't have read the surreal emails from my clients when I land them a feature in *Vogue*, *Forbes*, or *Shape Magazine*.

Fear would have stolen all of that. Every last drop of those accomplishments. Imagine what it has stolen from you already, what alternate reality could have been played out had fear not negotiated with you to stay small and comfortable. Imagine the capability it has to take from the part of your life that hasn't played out yet? The part that starts in this moment.

While I don't negotiate with fear, I also am realistic about the fact that fear keeps me comfortable, and to act against its wishes means I am going to get uncomfortable. That discomfort has allowed me to create, grow, and thrive. It has given me perspective and depth. It has given me all those accomplishments I listed above that I am immensely proud of.

So, fuck fear. Accept discomfort. Accomplish cool things.

But I know it is not that easy. It's not that easy because your mind is thinking and making circles around potential outcomes and hypothetical situations of where things could go wrong. It is ruminating on that first step while staying within the confines of pre-execution excitement. You are in the idea phase and that idea loves living in your mind.

And that is the entire problem—that your idea loves living in your mind, cozying up with daydreaming and magical lands. It is like a 25-year-old who won't leave their parents' house—and not because they are trying to save money for their super cool startup. Fear keeps you thinking about starting something or changing something in your business so much that you forget step two: to take action. If we can think a little less and act a little more, we will see progress starting to take form. Write down in your notes, on your to-do list, or wherever you keep your productivity organized, and put down one step you can take toward extracting this idea from your head and birthing it into your physical reality. When you're looking to diminish fear, know that its enemy is execution.

If paralysis just visited you and thoughts such as, "What step should I even take?" started flying around your mind and dominating your emotions, then let's start with a micro step. Here are a few action steps to take that are small, manageable, and will inspire you to start executing.

- Pick a name for your business—make it fun,create a poll, and send it to your closest friends and family to get their opinion
- Make a separate Instagram account for your business
- Secure the domain for your business website
- Create a Pinterest board and start pinning images that inspire you for the aesthetic of your brand

In the beginning, the more micro steps you can dream up and execute upon, the better. And don't forget to celebrate each step and have fun! Extracting the idea from your mind and into this world is one of the most exciting steps of starting your own business.

Fear might still visit when your idea is living in the wild—on Instagram, through a website, in the form of a meeting with a manufacturer. It has less say, though, at that point, because something finally exists outside of you. Other people are involved, if only from the vantage point that they know your idea exists. Fear can't put its grip on your creations so tightly anymore because its borders aren't the parameters of your brain.

Even though we are working on acting without it, fear is this completely natural and helpful emotion. It's also not entirely necessary at every step in our lives. At some point, it would be nice if we steered the ship of our lives without deferring to the imaginary and catastrophic weather report we make up in our minds.

So, I'll say it again: Fuck fear. Accept discomfort. Accomplish cool things.

The Lesson: Fear will always come up. You can let it say hello but never give it a vote at the table.

YOU ARE SAFE IN YOUR EMOTIONS.

Lesson #4:

Emotional Independence Is Where It's At

"Showing up for yourself and being your own biggest fan is healthy for our souls. Think of your soul as a bank and appreciating your wins is a way to deposit a credit into your soul bank. This allows you to be able to give to others, whether that may be giving your energy and appreciation to your staff, your patients, or your loved ones. Protect the energy that is your right to have and share it with others positively to help yourself achieve new success, as well as be a light to others in your life."

-Dr. Sheila Nazarian, Board Certified Plastic Surgeon, Mom, Entrepreneur, Activist

Out of all of my chakras, my root chakra is the most destabilized. My energy healer and intuitive-mindset coach are always telling me I need to ground myself through meditation or walks on the beach, rooting my bare feet to the soil of the earth. My foundation can be an open portal where I am flinging emotions at every angle, hoping something sticks toward healing. Within this chaotic space, I have this inherent emotional pattern where I act as if I cannot hold myself.

When you don't trust yourself with your foundation, you outsource it, which I did for years with swift mastery. In my early and mid-twenties, I believed that my emotions were too great of a burden to bear. When anxiety crept up my throat, it crippled me so much that I would grab my phone and text everyone close to me—my husband, my dad, my mom, my sister, my friends—letting them know the state of my emotions and that it was an emergency, and I just couldn't handle it anymore.

And then, they would come to my rescue—leaving work, stepping out of a meeting to take my call, picking me up to distract me, or making me my favorite foods. I surrendered to their care and love, like a child begging to enter the warm womb again. I served my emotions on a shitty plate and asked that they please hold them. And they did. Time after time. I got used to the attention.

I was in such a dark place that it wasn't yet possible for me to understand the well of strength that existed within. I hadn't met that strength yet or come to trust her. I didn't even know it existed. Instead, I hurt those around me in an effort to blind myself to how utterly helpless I was.

I recognized the urgent need to be able to hold myself emotionally after seeing the burden my husband was carrying as he attempted to follow his dreams, handle his emotions, and care for mine. Once I saw the years of struggle he was housing from my mental health, I quickly learned that being able to hold yourself in times of turmoil is so much more empowering than tossing it off to someone else. It will also lift loads of burdens of anxiety and worry from your loved ones so that they can get back to fulfilling their highest paths.

Finally, I woke up to my emotions and the effects they were having on others the moment my husband came home one day during a period where suicidal ideation wrecked my thoughts. His face was tethered from anxiety and he expressed that he was scared to come home out of fear that I wouldn't be alive anymore. The emotions I was offsetting to him were progressively diminishing his light. I had placed a thought, a fear, a potential reality into his head that I consciously would have never chosen for him. I looked at the stark reality of what my emotional turmoil was doing in the face of the one person I had chosen to live a life with, that I had promised a beautiful life to. I decided to take radical emotional responsibility over my bipolar disorder.

I wrote YOU ARE SAFE IN YOUR EMOTIONS on a pink Post-It note and pasted it to my bathroom mirror, which I looked at every day, numerous times a day. I started with that affirmation as a kind of contract with myself—to see how far I could go to truly believe that sentence. What opened up was a well of strength and a foundation I had so carelessly discarded and passed off to other people. After multiple sessions with my mindset coach, listening to Sarah Blondin on the Insight Timer App, journaling ferociously, and developing a spiritual practice, I found my center and was learning to finally cultivate emotional independence.

People always talk about *financial* independence. They want to be financially able to stand on their own two feet without the help of family members or government assistance. They strive, day after day, working tirelessly to smell that sweet freedom of being debt-free with a budget they can indulge themselves with.

But what about *emotional* independence? What about striving for the ability to stand on your own two feet to say, I CAN DO THIS NO MATTER WHAT?

Once you feel safe in your emotions, you will be able to swiftly move through fear and get a return from your pain. You will walk through experiences with your head held high, confident in your strength. You will inherently know that you can handle all of this. Emotional independence has no room for giving up or this *"I can't do it anymore"* narrative. It doesn't have room for playing the victim or wallowing in the deck of cards you were given. It also doesn't have room for numbing uncomfortable feelings.

You don't have to have a mental illness to know that there are parts of your life that you currently believe are too difficult to deal with. In that avoidance, there is a part of you that does not believe you can handle those emotions. What if, instead of knowing that there are aspects of life's emotional experience that you cannot handle, do not want to handle, and will avoid at all costs, you were able to look at your feelings and know that each one of them is a guide, a sign, and a mentor? What if you could wake up and not be afraid of how you might feel during any given moment? What if you just knew you could be there for yourself?

Feeling safe in your emotions is a daily practice, both proactively and reactively. To start the process of feeling safe in your emotions, you have to identify where you have survived. With the worksheet on the next page or in your personal journal, write down every painful challenge you have ever experienced (keep these short, 1-2 sentences per experience) and document the most prominent emotion you felt in that moment.

For each adversary, ask yourself, "Did I survive this?" The answer is yes, you did. I know this because you are reading this book and are able to tell the tale of that challenging experience.

Next, under each hardship, write, "I survived this and am stronger because…" Don't cop out on the "stronger because" moment because that is where the magic happens.

Challenge #1:

> *Did I survive this?* _____

> *I survived this and am stronger because*

Challenge #2:

> *Did I survive this?* _____

> *I survived this and am stronger because*

Challenge #3:

Did I survive this? _____

I survived this and am stronger because

[   ]

I want you to soak this in for a moment. In the moments you thought your heart was being physically ripped from your body and that your blood would stop pumping through your veins, you survived, and a different narrative played out.

Your emotions paint the color of the external circumstances that happen around and to you. You have also, for as many years as you have been breathing on this planet, survived each and every one of those emotions. Which simply means, if you did it once, you can do it again. Knowing you can survive takes the fear out of the equation, or at least adds in a willingness to compose yourself with grace and faith when another adversary comes your way.

Once you have written down all of your hardships and logged your survival evidence, write down twice as many moments when you were brimming with love, happiness, and fulfillment. This serves as evidence that other emotions and experiences exist that fill our cups and color our lives so vibrantly. These are the moments to remember when you are sludging through the quicksand and are not convinced beauty still exists.

Love-Filled Moment #1:

[   ]

Happy Moment #2:

[ ]

Fulfilling Moment #3:

[ ]

Even though you have all of this evidence logged to create this foundation of feeling safe in your emotions, emotions can be highly potent and need further soothing at times. If you are in a moment of complete chaos, urgency, depression, or anxiety, soak in any number of these following practices—whichever one(s) that are calling you forward:

1. *Identify that you are feeling unsafe.* The first step to feeling safe within the emotion you are feeling is to identify that it is present and flowing around your mind. Uncomfortable emotions often come from resisting what we are actually trying to feel. Anxiety stems from trying to resist anxiety. Fear brims from trying to resist fear. Instead, say, "I am feeling anxiety right now." Identifying and accepting whatever you are feeling allows you to assess the situation with more clarity.

2. *Witness your emotions without judgment.* When we are feeling anxious or depressed, we often think we are one with that emotion. If we can sit still and witness our emotions as a third-party bystander, we separate ourselves from the anxiety or depression. In this witnessing however, we must

1. observe without judgment. We usually jump to make uncomfortable feelings wrong with thoughts like, "I shouldn't be feeling this way" or "I am not strong enough to experience this right now." Taking away that layer of judgment allows us to experience the emotion for what it is—just a human experience that will leave our bodies in due time. Rid yourself from its negative charge and just witness how it feels in your body.

2. *Get rid of any victimhood narrative.* Wallowing in the "why me?" aspect of feeling an uncomfortable emotion is like adding wind to a wildfire. You are packing on layers of suffering that will lead you deeper and deeper into destructive management and chaos. When your mind is trying to make you the victim, shift the narrative and imagine yourself as the queen of the scenario.

3. *Give thanks to your emotions.* If you are feeling an emotion—any emotion—that means you are alive. Even in the depths of negativity, that deserves a moment of gratitude. Thank your emotion for visiting you and acting as an alert for something external influencing your life. Thank it for giving you the opportunity to show how strong you can be in its presence. Thank it for providing you another test that proves you are alive.

4. *Remind yourself that this will pass.* Often when our emotions are thick and heavy, we believe they will be present forever. We have to remind ourselves in the most intense of experiences that these emotions will move through us and we will be restored back to homeostasis—or something even better!

5. *Visualize your root chakra strengthening.* Your root chakra sits at the base of your spine. Imagine your pelvic floor acting like a pot where your spine grows. Imagine rich soil and a steady foundation. Breathe into that pot and trust that it knows how

to hold and grow all of you.

6. *Move energy.* Now that you have identified, witnessed without judgment, reminded yourself of the fleeting nature of emotions, ditched the victimhood mindset, repeated a mantra, and visualized your foundation strengthening through your root chakra, it is time to move energy. Moving energy can look so many different ways. If your emotion is chaotic, take a deep breath and scream into a pillow. If you need to calm your energy, get into a downward facing dog and take a few breaths or go for a leisurely walk around the block. If you need to get your energy OUT, throw a few punches into the air, do some jumping jacks, take a run, or furiously write in your journal everything that comes to mind.

7. *Give yourself a hug.* And I mean a real, physical hug. Wrap your arms around your body, close your eyes, and whisper, "I love you." Sometimes, when we feel unsafe in our emotions, it is an opportunity to provide so much love to ourselves. Sometimes, we just need to be reminded of the love we have to give and receive.

This is how I maintain or at least hold on to my commitment to my emotional independence. I talk to my emotions out loud and acknowledge their presence. I thank them for the visit and ask them to reveal why they are here. I know they will pass because no feeling is final. I hold on to a vision of purpose, inspiration, and intention that I bask in the other 75% of my day.

This is not to say that you should not reach out in times of need or overwhelm. We all need a support system and a friend to vent to on particularly hard days. Emotional independence just means that you know, despite whatever comes your way, that you've got this, and that when uncomfortable emotions come up, you can check in with yourself before seeking external support.

For the rest of your days, you've got this. And from that beautiful belief stems the confidence to get back to building and living within your creation.

The Lesson: Take responsibility for your emotions and learn how to always be the net that catches you when you fall.

WE ARE ALL CO-CREATING OUR LIVES WITH AN UNSEEN, GREATER FORCE AT HAND.

Lesson #5

Uncertainty is the Only Guarantee

"As the old saying goes, the only thing constant in life is change. Being your own boss is the dream but it requires the ability to adapt and being able to pivot at a moment's notice. To look at an obstacle from all angles. Anytime you take a big leap, especially in the business world, you are unsure of the ground you're going to land on and uncertainty is inevitable. Learn to be malleable and comfortable with the unknown by surrendering to the flow of your business."

-Natalie Holloway, co-founder of Bala

My first hire was my best friend. It was both an exhilarating and terrifying process. I had always lovingly joked about her being my first employee, but we both thought that would be years down the line, not months after I secured my first client with Scout's Agency. But there we were, sitting at a sushi restaurant even though she doesn't like fish, drinking a beer, and me giving her a job offer.

Being responsible for another individual's salary and financial state felt daunting, heavy, and very adult. Couple that with the fact that I loved her and her husband dearly felt in alignment for me—if anyone was going to reap the rewards of my business, I was happy to have it be someone close to me.

And so, I hired her. Mostly because it sounded fun and also because I had gained 10 clients in four months, was making more than I had ever made, and wanted to turn the dial up significantly. I have been told that I leap and pray that a parachute appears.

As I hired her, I also signed a year lease for the office of my dreams; a concrete, modern storefront loft with floor-to-ceiling windows that sat on the outskirts of Little Italy, my favorite borough of San Diego. My other best friend lived in the building, another was walking distance to the office, and happy hours were abundantly penciled into our Google calendar at flourishing restaurants down the block where decor over food was most likely the intention.

It was all lining up: I opened up an LLC, hired my first employee, signed a lease to an office, purchased tickets to a conference, and was gleamingly and optimistically off to the races in my business.

And then, like a swift shudder of a sword, uncertainty paid me a visit. I lost four large clients within one week before we were ever able to replenish the client roster for her to start working on. For the next few months, all the incoming cash was going toward paying the bills—since I created overhead for myself with an office—and paying her salary. I took home two, maybe three thousand a month, lived off my savings, watched that personal account that I shared with my husband dwindle down to almost nothing. I wasn't dialing down my lifestyle that I had grown accustomed to, and I wasn't being honest about my books. I was avoiding reality while also throwing spaghetti at a wall in an attempt to see which clients would stick. It was chaotic and stressful, and I am grateful that I was able to see the lesson in this challenge because it shaped my future as an entrepreneur.

I recovered and came back by doubling my revenue (which came from a shift in mindset from scarcity to abundance—more on that later), but the point of this anecdote is that one moment I was flying high, sure of the outcome of the coming months, to sitting in financial distress the next which seeped into all areas of my life, including my marriage. I was scrambling for clients, desperate for cash, and learning a wonderfully heavy lesson: nothing is for certain, and as the steerer of the ship, you are the one that takes on that uncertainty.

But let's not live in fear. Uncertainty sounds scary and daunting. It sounds all encompassing, as if we don't have a say in the trajectory of our life; as if we are victims to external circumstances that can come, at any point, and take our achievements away. This isn't true and it is true. Major external circumstances can come and change the name of the game. We saw this tragically with COVID-19 and the effects it had on small businesses across the world. The goal here, in an ever-changing world where uncertainty and change are the only constants, is to learn how to dance in uncertainty and not lose your step mid-waltz, but rather wow yourself with your landing.

We are all co-creating our lives with an unseen, greater force at hand. There were many things I did that put myself in a compromising situation where I was forced to take financial cutbacks at a time when I was not in a position to do so. My clients were on month-to-month contracts meaning future planning was near to impossible. Regardless of not having a time frame commitment from my clients, I hired someone, not knowing if I would be able to pay her over the months - I just knew I could pay her that month and the month after that. Regardless of bringing on a large new expense, an employee, I also bound myself to a lease. I paid for us to attend a conference. I decorated the office. I bought us matching jumpsuits and business cards and flyers that we never handed out. I did all of these things all at once without too much of a foundation. And so, I got kicked in the ass.

There are things I do now to ensure more certainty in my business. Without these small metrics, it would be very difficult to maintain inner peace and financial confidence for both my personal life and the health of my agency. My clients now sign three to six month contracts so that I can predict future income flow. With that, I can budget appropriately on extra expenses or additional team members. I can see the amount of revenue the business will bring in next month, the month after, and for another six months. With those numbers, I know when I need to add in new clients and give myself appropriate lead time to land those deals through sales. My payroll system automatically pays me a salary - one that I feel comfortable taking from the business every month. With that, I am able to budget my life with my husband.

But this is the foundation that I built and worked diligently to create. In the beginning, the future is always highly uncertain. Your next client or next sale isn't guaranteed (it never is actually), until you get into a rhythm where the business begins to breathe and have its own life force. This uncertainty is the reason so many people do not take the jump to pursue the work they have been yearning to pursue. They cannot walk away from their secure paycheck that they know will be deposited into their bank accounts twice a month. They cannot let go of that safety they feel, knowing they can budget their life appropriately. They do not take into account that with that safety net comes so many pitfalls: they cannot increase their salary whenever they want, they are placing faith in another human being, the CEO, that the ship is running smoothly and will run smoothly for the foreseeable future, and they cannot guarantee they won't be laid off at a moment's notice.

The road that feels safe is also uncertain.

Once you take a step back and realize that no aspect of life is guaranteed (except change) is the moment life becomes freeing. Uncertainty just shows up through different images depending on different life choices - and no one is exempt from its wrath. As you decide to craft and mold and paint the life and career you are ready to create, know that you are co-creating so you get the privilege of being ready when uncertainty hits.

When uncertainty does come knocking on the door, employ the following emotional hacks to act from a foundational place instead of an anxious one:

1. *Exhibit the energy of a calm person.* Sometimes in chaos, we can jump ahead four or five steps into total catastrophe. As an entrepreneur, you will need to look uncertainty in the eye with a calm, level headed demeanor so that you can implement strategy and actions that will work. Before you react hastily, take a step back, take a few deep breaths and try to exhibit the energy of a calm person. Make decisions out of this rooted place.

2. *Have goals but not expectations.* The moment you expect the sale or the monthly revenue or the sold out launch is the moment uncertainty will pay you a visit when anything but that bottom line is hit. Have manifestations and have goals, but release the expectations of the number that will come to you eventually. Dream the dream and then detach from the outcome.

3. *Expect uncertainty.* Oftentimes, we can deal with the chaos if

we consciously realize we have decided to let it into our lives. As an entrepreneur, you are signing an invisible contract that guarantees situations to unfold that you were not prepared for or did not expect. If you can go into your business expecting the unpredictable to happen at one point or another, you won't be caught like a deer in headlights but rather you will recognize the call and step up to the plate.

(4.) *Think of uncertainty as the ticket.* If you re-frame your relationship to uncertainty as the visitor that knights you as an entrepreneur, you won't act out of complete fear when it knocks on your door. You will smile and say, "I knew you would come!" And then move on knowing that you are officially an entrepreneur.

Fall in love with uncertainty because in that space creativity can endlessly flow, preconceived limits aren't real, boundaries of what you think you are capable of can be expanded. And even though it all pours onto your shoulders as the entrepreneur, you also have the ability to look at that responsibility as a great honor - the honor of crafting your own life.

The Lesson: Live in uncertainty's discomfort: there you will find the root of all future abundance.

DO NOT THINK THAT YOU ARE SPECIAL. YOU ARE LIKE ALL OF US—YOU ALSO HAVE A VOICE, A POINT OF VIEW, AND A PERSPECTIVE THAT WE ARE WAITING FOR YOU TO SHARE.

Lesson #6:

You Are The Only One Who Can Do This, But You Don't Have To Do It All Alone

"Build a network of champions who will rally around your mission. When your business transforms into a team sport, that's when the magic really happens."

-Trinity Mouzon Wofford, co-founder of Golde

This lesson is two-fold, so stay with me here.

ACT ONE: IT IS YOU AND ONLY YOU

Every breath, syllable uttered, and physical step has brought you to the moment where you developed an idea of something you can do, become, or produce. The custom roadmap of countless little decisions you have made, phases you have gone through as a teenager, cities you have lived in, and friend groups you have had has crescendoed you into this moment where you have declared your business idea. Your cumulative experience is your credibility. It is the reason that the words you speak, the logo you choose, and the mission statement of your business is uniquely yours. You are what sets the entire operation and brand apart.

Yet, regardless of the magic in all of that—the fact that if you had chosen the apartment with the back patio over the apartment with the second bathroom, your life would have taken a different course—you still might be asking yourself, *"This has been done before. What do I have to bring to the table?"*

Influencers run rampant on social media, business courses are being sold by the thousands, authors sprout up left and right, a new skincare line is dropped consistently, and motivational speakers fill the bios of Instagram users.

And yet despite the so-called "saturation," they all still find their audience.

The spirituality market is a great example. I follow numerous spiritual leaders, from Sahara Rose to Gabby Bernstein to Wayne Dyer. I read their books, listen to their podcasts, and follow them on social media. Their message at the end of the day is the same and quite pure, but the nuances in which they speak them—Sahara with her ferocious dances on TikTok, Gabby with her calm yet direct storytelling, Wayne with his comprehensive and woo-woo concepts—light me up in different ways. Without each of my spiritual teachers, I am not sure my connection to The Universe would be complete. I need to learn how to use my body to dance sacred movements like Sahara, I need to learn to trust The Universe like Gabby, and I need to learn the philosophical meanings behind these spiritual philosophies like Wayne.

And these are just three examples. There are so many more I look to on a daily basis to ignite different areas of my spiritual practice.

And thank God for them all because if one of them looked at the market, looked at the books that had already been published and the Instagrams that had already been started, one of them might not have even begun and that would have robbed the world of their gifts, healing, and inspiration. It would have robbed me from the individual perspectives they each bring, which have colored my life with purpose and connection. It would have robbed me of the lessons I learned from them and have implemented into my daily life for the better.

If they didn't rob this world of their gifts, who are you to consider such a route? Who are you to say your voice does not matter? That others are already doing this? Who are you to say that the exact way you want to do things is not valid? Who are you to say that you are a fraud when you, as a living human being, have a collection of experiences, emotions, traumas, and joys that, if told, will speak to another member of the collective?

Do not think that you are special. You are like all of us—you also have a voice, a point of view, and a perspective that we are waiting for you to share. Stand deep into your personal power when building your product, course, or podcast because it is in that power that your business will succeed.

What is your personal power? Your personal power is the zone in which you feel excitement and flow. You know you are in it when you wake up with an energetic pull to create the thing that previously lived in your mind. You gladly record a podcast or write a chapter of your book. You gladly take meeting after meeting with different manufacturers to see who is the perfect fit to develop your skincare line. You do not show up in a state of resistance. You show up in a state of eager action.

When you find that energetic pull, do not be so foolish as to diminish it under the false pretenses that you are not unique enough in the space. You as a living entity are proof of uniqueness. Do not look at the living proof and negate it out of fear and insecurity. Push through and trust your personal power.

Your being already knows your personal power—it is just waiting for you to get quiet enough to listen to it. In the spirit of finding it so that we can live in it, here is a worksheet that can activate the introduction to your personal power. Don't overthink it. She lives within you already and has been waiting to meet you.

Finding Your Personal Power

What is one activity you are excited to do without getting paid for it?

_____

_____

When you are in the flow of this activity, how do you feel?

_____

_____

What does it feel like when you are doing a task that you are in a state of resistance around?

_____

_____

What is the difference between these two feelings?

_____

How can you implement that activity of flow, where your personal power is on display, into the messaging or the structure of your business?

ACT TWO: The Two Types of Support

HIRING SUPPORT

As you dance and play within your personal power, you will start to weave your business into reality. Things will start to take form: your website, social media channels, business emails, Shopify page, sample products, blog posts. You will be the CEO, the CFO, the marketing director, the customer service agent, and the distribution operations.

You might get to a point, within all of the hat wearing, where you feel that your business is expanding to the level where you need support. The dance between the hats has been fruitful—it allowed you to place your unique stamp on all departments—but at some point, within our personal power, we must come to the supportive truth that we cannot do it alone.

Support within our business comes in two forms: actual team members that are responsible for an aspect of your business and a support system that is there for you emotionally.

Hiring team members, whether they are freelance independent contractors or full-time employees, can be a nerve wracking first jump. Every time I hire a new employee, I physically want to vomit for 24 hours. The pressure of being responsible for someone else's full time salary is daunting. I have also done it and therefore have gotten used to that level of business management. Now, I can do it again and again and again when my business needs it. In the beginning, however, it can be difficult to bring in team members because of two different aspects: 1) the financial responsibility of supporting them and 2) giving up control over every little task.

When it comes to the financial responsibility, every business has different cash flow and every business owner has different ways of managing that cash. Setting aside money for support is the best thing you can do for the overall health of your business and for you. If you are used to profiting all of your revenue as a solopreneur, start playing with the idea that if you put a percentage of that monthly revenue away for support (which can be anything from editing your podcast episodes to taking over customer service emails) that then frees up time in your calendar to focus on bigger picture strategies like how to increase streams of revenue or how to grow your audience.

You do not have to do every minute task yourself. In fact, getting too bogged down as the steerer of the ship in daily tasks at a certain point in your business is counterproductive to the entire brand growing. You set up the systems, now let someone else play in them so that you can look to future growth and map out the next phase of your business.

When bringing on support for your business, it is important that the people you bring into your space are those that align with three things: 1) your work culture 2) value added by the employee and 3) your business values.

1. *Your Work Culture:* The way you play in business is the way you are going to want others to play with you. For example, do you want a work culture that is more flexible or stricter with the daily rules? Beyond the exchange of money for labor, what type of community do you want to build within your business? If you are looking for a laid back environment

where your employees are empowered to have a self-employed mindset, you are going to hire someone very different than if you were looking to build a very corporate, rational, and output based environment. This is where things get exciting, because as the entrepreneur, you get to create your work culture. So ask yourself, What is my ideal work culture? As you interview, make sure your new addition to the team wants to live within that same environment. It is a sure way for your employees to be fulfilled beyond their daily tasks.

2. *Value Added By The Employee:* Support for your business, especially in the beginning when you haven't scaled to a full on team, should always come with enormous value added. The person you bring on should contribute to supporting you with your workload by taking certain tasks off of your plate or contributing directly to an increase in revenue for your business. The value has to be rich for you, especially with your first few hires.

3. *Your Business Values:* Do you want your company to have a no gossip policy? Do you want your employees to treat your customers from a place of empathy and love? Take some time to think about the values you want your company to stand for and when hiring support, make sure that they are not only aligned with your business values but also extremely stoked to live them out on a daily basis.

EMOTIONAL SUPPORT

You also do not have to emotionally walk down the entrepreneurship path alone. As stated in every letter and page of this book, the entrepreneurial path is an emotional one and if you do not have a business partner, it can also be a lonely one. Every entrepreneur needs a support system to hype them up, listen to them vent from time to time, and cheer them on from the sidelines.

In the beginning of starting Scout's Agency, I relied on my husband, which in hindsight was not a healthy dynamic for either of us. I was having a lot of difficulty being able to handle client relations. My days were struck if a client sent me an email that was anything but enthusiastic around my services and in return, I came home and unloaded my fears, anxieties, and stress on my husband in hopes that he would provide me with the comfort to keep going.

This unhealthy dynamic was put on full display when we were taking a trip to Italy together. Our first trip abroad as a couple, just the two of us. The moment the airplane landed in Italy, my phone notified me of an email from a client that was anything but favorable. My body froze , my heart began to race, and my entire being went into panic mode. The beginning of our trip was completely shot as I was unable to get out of the emergency feeling that I had done something wrong (which I now have the hindsight and confidence to proclaim that I hadn't, and there are times in business where no matter what you do, you cannot please the other).

I remember being at a world famous butcher's restaurant in a small town off the beaten path in Tuscany that we had gone out of our way to visit. We were sitting sampling the highest quality beef tartares I had ever had the pleasure of eating. Yet, the anxiety I was feeling around my business—an unfavorable email from a demanding client, not knowing if I was working enough and serving my clients properly while on vacation, and feeling alone in the situation as the entrepreneur—overpowered the extremely special moment that I should have been sharing with my husband. I excused myself, walked down an alley of the small town, and cried my eyes out.

In other words, my inability to hold myself in business began to weigh on him heavily. I was living my dream, yes, but client relations and being responsible for my monthly income and the majority of our livelihood (he is actively getting his PhD) was an emotional challenge I had yet to master. And so, I flung my chaotic emotions onto him as I had done in the past with my bipolar disorder.

Support systems are there for support but they are not there to hold our entire beings up. That is our job. They are there to infuse us with strength and remind us of our confidence when we momentarily forget. A support system is needed however to know that you are not doing this alone, that there are people out there that love you and support you, and on those days when you especially can't see the progress, having a girlfriend remind you of your accomplishments is key.

I love talking to the girlfriends in my life that are also entrepreneurs. If none of your friends run their own thing, there are so many local entrepreneurial groups that host meet-ups and events. If virtual is preferred, Facebook has a plethora of groups where entrepreneurs can come together for advice and support (you can also join The Emotional Entrepreneur group on the Geneva app! Go to: bit.ly/scoutcommunity or get the link at my Instagram bio @scoutsobel to join us!). Seek out mentors who are further along in the game that you can go to in particularly challenging moments. Follow your favorite entrepreneurs on Instagram. Community around entrepreneurship is more readily available and at your fingertips than ever before. All you need to do is invite yourself in, reach out to a friend, and know that people want to see you succeed.

You are the only one who can build your business but you do not have to do it alone.

The Lesson: You deserve support as you build the life of your dreams.

UNPOPULAR OPINION: YOUR ANXIETY HAS YOUR BACK.

Lesson #7:

Your Anxiety Is Trying To Tell You Something

"If something is making me feel anxious, doesn't bring me joy, and doesn't serve me, I back away from the situation. Listening to my anxiety is an amazing gift. I now know, after living with anxiety from a young age, that it is always trying to tell me something."

-Charlotte McKinney, Actress and Model

Unpopular opinion: Your anxiety has your back.

Granted, sometimes the execution is a bit inflated and exaggerated, but at the root of those heart palpitations, vibrating sensations throughout your muscles, and general panic soaring throughout each of your cells is a purpose and a function—the warning sign. This warning sign will throw its hands up over and over and over again as you become an entrepreneur or leap into the unknown to find your fulfillment. If you break it down simply, anxiety is the signal that you are out of your comfort zone. And I can say from the view I experience every day: Welcome. We have been waiting for you.

When you take a leap to change your life, start a new one, or jump into a venture that doesn't come with a guarantee of success, your mind is entering new territory every day as if you were a straggler in a large, deep forest attempting to find your way amongst the redwoods and the critters. New circumstances will be flung your way every moment; new animals, and plants, and sounds. The goal is not to get out of the forest but learn how to live within it.

I have lived with anxiety that has crippled me and overtaken both my mind and my body for the majority of my life here on this planet. It has taken things from me: my college experience, jobs, internships, opportunities, memories with family and friends, a trip to Paris (still not over that one), the peace and happiness of my loved ones, my sense of self, my sense of an ambitious future, the dream, at times, that I would become anything. I lived with it on a daily basis for over fifteen years and with my bipolar diagnosis it became just another medical symptom. People would ask me what I was anxious about and I would say, Nothing. It's a chemical imbalance. There's nothing I can do about it.

But that narrative wasn't true. My brain plummeted me into a deep, deep swimming pool at a young age without the tools to even tread water. That is a reason to be anxious—or at least live with a sense of panic. My mother was diagnosed with Multiple Sclerosis when I was 14. That is a reason to be anxious. My parents got divorced at the age of 17. That is a reason to be anxious. My therapist told me I was flirting between chronic and clinical depression when I was 16. That is a reason to be anxious. In a world of private schools and my peers getting to Ivy League schools, I didn't get into any colleges, not even my safety. That is a reason to be anxious. I developed a sense of paranoia that men were following me home, on my balcony, beneath my bed, hiding in my closet waiting to hurt me. That is a reason to be anxious. The doctors put me on a 51/50 hold in the hospital. That is a reason to be anxious. I was told that I needed to be monitored for the rest of my life because my mental illness was so severe, I could become unstable at any moment. That is a reason to be anxious.

Couple all of those specific anecdotes with the patriarchy, society's need for us to be constantly busy and distracted by scrolling feeds, gender cages, racial and social injustice, body image standards, the "shoulds" of the world, and parental expectations, amongst others, and yeah, I would say we have a few reasons to be anxious.

When I started working with my mindset coach, she would ask me over and over and over again until I could come up with any sort of answer about why I was feeling anxious. I learned that despite my denial, there is always a why. It might be so general or engrained or repressed within us but it is there. When anxiety visits us, it is always telling us a profound message: Something is out of alignment here. You are not in your true state: creativity, flow, ease, peace. Something within isn't right. Something external is affecting you. You are acting within the realms of fear. You are entering new territory.

They say the entrepreneur is always putting out the fires; a problem at the warehouse, cleaning up an employee's error, calming an upset client, losing a revenue stream, troubleshooting the website. Everything that can happen will happen to you as you start up the business of your dreams, things you didn't plan for and margins of error you did. There will be tangible fires to put out, ones with distinct actionable items: call the warehouse, call the IT girl, apologize to the client, etc. Then, there will be fires that are so abstract because they are growing in your mind.

I had to get really good at managing my anxiety in the early stages of my business. Around month three, a relationship with a client had grown sour. Since I was in the very early stages, I didn't have the confidence or the awareness to know that I get to choose who I work with and who enters my space. I don't have to cling to every client because they pay me. If our working styles clash or if they don't respect my process or services, then we can part ways respectfully regardless of the contract's initial duration. So I clinged on and cried numerous times and worked twice as hard to prove it to her—now I know I could have never really proved it to her—and I still couldn't repair the relationship.

Within that experience, a lot of things were testing me personally. I have always been a people pleaser and I consider it one of my weaknesses. People pleasing has taken over my schedule, energy levels, and inner fulfillment. It was (and still is) a weakness of mine I had always wanted to work on but felt it too painful to sit in the discomfort of others if I knew I could jump in and save some part of their day. My agency forced me to examine this trait in myself and work on it—quickly. I remember waiting for the elevator to go up to my apartment one day and laughing to myself. *I, the biggest people pleaser of all, started a service based agency where client relations is my job. I hear you, God. I know what I need to do.*

I was constantly anxious because I was put out of my comfort zone and as entrepreneurship always tends to do, my business was illuminating a personal area of growth I needed to confront quickly. So, my anxiety let me know—over and over and over again in those beginning months—that I was a) out of my comfort zone and b) I had to work on some shit to not feel completely off balanced in this new territory. The universe gave me no choice: work on this or get swallowed by your business.

The point here is that anxiety isn't this thing to just get rid of, skip over, and aim to never have. Yes, it is uncomfortable and I could think of a handful of other emotions I would rather be experiencing but what if, just for a few minutes, we said hello when anxiety visited and listened to its cry? What if we knew that anxiety was visiting because it was either a warning sign—YOU ARE ENTERING UNKNOWN TERRITORY. BEWARE AND SUIT UP!—or it was telling us something wasn't in alignment for us—THIS ISN'T FOR YOUR HIGHEST GOOD AND YOU AREN'T ACTING OUT OF AUTHENTICITY. REASSESS AND CHANGE COURSE. Either way, it's a magical compass that if we listened to more often, we could course correct our days, deal with ingrained toxic patterns like people pleasing, and learn how to put out those fires without our centers unraveling into deep chaos.

Viewing anxiety as a magical compass helps us reframe our perspective but it still does not provide us with the tools to navigate and steer the ship using that compass. I view my anxiety upkeep into two buckets: preventative and present. A lot of times, anxiety is the warning sign that visits after you have experienced the trigger repeatedly over time. Therefore, if anxiety is the thing that finally tells us to stop or that danger is around the corner, there are things we can do to prevent the visit of heart palpitations and catastrophic dread. Honing in on your peace muscle will allow you to rely on it when something does finally crescendos or better yet, reduce the chance of an emergency like state even coming about in the first place.

Building your peace muscle means reducing the daily tasks and habits that raise your cortisol levels and distract you from your foundational core. If you can implement moments of peace into your day, especially in the beginning and the end, your anxiety has less of a ladder to climb. It won't have moments to feast upon to explode with later. It will get the message that you are safe here.

Ways to build your peace muscle outside of work:

Put your phone away for large chunks of time: I am a huge advocate for putting your phone away an hour before bed, not looking at your phone for the first hour of your morning, and putting it away for your thirty-minute lunch. High performing entrepreneurs adopt this practice. Arianna Huffington puts her phone away before bed and does not check it first thing in the morning and Lauryn Evarts Bosstick from The Skinny Confidential goes up to two hours every morning without checking her phone. Not only do the notifications, texts, emails, and social media apps cause distraction and overwhelm, studies have also shown that screen time is correlated with a decrease in sleep quality. Being plugged in constantly does not allow your mind a break. Without breaks, your mind runs on the hamster wheel inducing anxiety. Finding times to consciously be without your phone will recenter you and ground you into your energy not the energy of rapid notifications.

Be in nature: Implement moments throughout your day where you put everything down, close the computer, walk outside, and just be. It has been said that nature is the shaman's medicine. Throughout my day, I make sure to step outside even for a few moments to take a deep breath and look up at the sky. Sometimes, I will just look around my backyard and study the trees, their roots, the way their branches form. If you are struggling to find ways in which you can get outside more, here are a few beautiful examples: go for a walk, do your at-home workout outside, eat your meals outside, meditate on your porch, balcony, or backyard, read outside, take your laptop and get emails done on the grass—the list goes on! Even if you just take one step outside for five minutes to breath each day, you will reap the benefits of being in nature.

Expressing gratitude: Expressing gratitude daily is one of the most purposeful things you can do to infuse your life with magic. The things you express gratitude for do not need to be large or grand. They can simply be, I am grateful for my cup of coffee this morning or I am grateful that my new book arrived in the mail or I am grateful that I have fresh veggies to eat for dinner tonight. I express gratitude in a plethora of ways. Sometimes, I write three things I am grateful for in my journal in the morning, other times I will put my hand over my heart and say them out loud, and when I need someone else to hold space for me in my gratitude, I will text my grateful list to my sister and ask her what she is grateful for. Expressing gratitude allows fear to take the backseat. The more you experience gratitude, the more your anxiety will be notified that you are in fact safe.

Implementing these three daily practices in your life will significantly increase your peace muscle but that doesn't mean that anxiety won't visit you at work, in a more lightning bolt kind of way. We now know that anxiety is our body trying to tell us something but that doesn't mean it needs to pay us a long visit. Let's welcome it in, get the message, implement new strategies, and allow its message to reroute.

Ways to build your peace muscle at work:

Stop and listen: When you start feeling anxious at work, put everything down, place your hands by your side, and just sit. Identify that you are anxious without any positive or negative judgments attached to that identification. Just breathe through the experience without thinking or feeling as if you shouldn't be feeling anything but what you are currently feeling.

Question its arrival: Once you have identified without judgment that anxiety has visited, question the purpose of its arrival. Was it something your employee said? Was it an email from an upset client? Did you find out your customers didn't receive their product? If you aren't coming up with any particular reason, keep deducing by asking yourself, What are you currently afraid of? Don't accept the answer of *I don't know*. Assess and assess and assess until you go layers deeper into the why of your fear.

Thank it for its visit: Express gratitude toward your anxiety! Thank it for coming. Without it, you wouldn't have the emotional trigger that it is time to either get into action or accept the things you cannot control. Either way, it is asking you to do something about an external situation. Without anxiety, you would never know when potential danger is on its way.

Take action: Now that you have identified your anxiety without judgment, found the root of why it is present, and expressed gratitude for it having your back, you get to take action. Sometimes, action looks like calling the warehouse to get the current status and emailing your disappointed customers with a 20% off coupon for their next purchase. Other times, it looks like collecting yourself to have a hard conversation with your employee. However taking action can also mean not taking action at all. My favorite prayer for anxiety is the serenity prayer:

> *God, grant me the serenity to accept the things I cannot change, courage to change the things I can, and the wisdom to know the difference.*

Before taking action, call upon this prayer to identify if you can change the current situation or if it is out of your control. If it is out of your control, for example when PEOPLE Magazine didn't pick up my client's launch story, I got to step back and say that I did everything that was under my control: wrote an amazing pitch and got it to the top editor, who then distributed it to her team. The decision for PEOPLE to pick it up was not in my hands. Therefore, anxiety around the outcome is tricking me into thinking the rejection was in my control. It was not. And when something is out of my control, I accept the fact that I did all I could do and the rest I get to let go. Anxiety will tell you otherwise since not being in control can send our human minds into chaos. Here is where you get to get super specific—is the situation you are anxious over in your control or out of your control? If it is in control, create a calm and rational plan of action and if it is out of YOUR control, you get to be grateful that you did your part and have faith that divine timing is at play.

As you start your new venture or as you are currently stepping into it, know that anxiety will come. Understand what you have signed up for and listen when you get the honor of it paying you a visit. The moment we stop suppressing anxiety's voice and instead start listening to its arrival in our bodies is the moment we start healing and becoming stronger within our personal lives and within our business. Once you end the war on anxiety and build up your daily peace muscle, it no longer needs to be constantly living within you. It trusts that you got it, that you can co-create your beautiful life with the universe and that you are assessing all of your external and internal factors and reactions. Suddenly, the moment you invite it in, it doesn't feel the need to stay. It's job is done.

The Lesson: When you accept that anxiety isn't the bad guy but ignoring it is, you get to face your circumstances head on and grow stronger every time you walk through the fire.

WHEN YOU MAKE A
DEAL WITH RISK, YOU
ALSO MAKE A DEAL
WITH MAGIC.

Lesson #8:

Risk Is Beautiful, But Don't Be Foolish

"When I moved to LA, I quit my job in digital marketing to pursue blogging full time, but I didn't plan realistically so I was in debt, burnt out, and I had to take another corporate job to pay the bills. It felt like a failure at the time, but it was a huge lesson that taught me how to set myself up smartly, save, and be patient, so that I did it right with Almost 30. My co-founder Lindsey and I built the business for two years while working our 9-to-5s, so when I finally quit my corporate job for good, I felt completely aligned and knew in my Soul it was the right move."

-Krista Williams, co-host of Almost 30 Podcast

My sister always says, *"Scout is the type of entrepreneur who jumps out of a plane and prays a parachute miraculously appears!"*

It's true. At a certain point, I stop the endless loop of analyzing potential outcomes and I leap, trusting that the parachute will open and hold me as I float toward success. I also leap trusting that if it doesn't, a lesson is waiting for me that will catapult me to the next level of my life. In other words, regardless of what happens to my life after I take a risk, I have a deep rooted belief that I will be okay no matter the outcome and that if that outcome is not favorable, I will dust myself off and emerge stronger. Therefore risk always brings me something: a success or a lesson.

In more business terms, I am not risk-averse to a point that it is probably masochistic.

Risk is the ticket price we pay to get into the game, into the arena, and into the land of creation. When we start taking responsibility for our lives and our careers and our relationships, we sign an invisible contract that states that we acknowledge we are taking on a level of risk to build what we envision in our mind and place it into the physical world.

Sometimes that risk is grand; leaving a comfy salary and financial safety that supports your family. Sometimes that risk is more subtle; potentially losing an opportunity because you decided to go in a different direction. Regardless of the scope of the risk, taking it means one thing: you value the things that light your soul up more than you value a societal safety net.

I encourage risk because it is the way to your highest path. I believe that when we are put in a position where we *have* to show up, where major things are on the line whether that's your income or your reputation, we show up gallantly in ways we never expected from ourselves. That point of pressure is what makes us stand tall and play big. With a willingness to show up no matter what and an infinite trust that your life is being played out in ways that support you living abundantly and within purpose, the needle of your life will move in the direction you desire regardless of the road bumps that come up along the way.

We have all seen the rewards that come from the greatest entrepreneurs of all times taking risks to start their businesses. Sara Blakely had $5,000 in her savings account when she decided to launch and create Spanx while working a stable 9-to-5 sales job. Blake Mycoskie, founder of TOMS, started his business with an entirely new business model of donating a pair of shoes to someone in need for each purchase. Tom and Lisa Bilyeu started Quest in the middle of the 2009 economic downfall which reached a $1 billion evaluation six years later. Oprah Winfrey dropped out of college to pursue a job offer in broadcasting.

See the pattern? In order to start something grand and beautiful and sustainable and fulfilling, it does start with a certain level of risk.

That being said, we don't need to be reckless within the course of our lives. Yes, taking big action despite risk will reap us great rewards but to enjoy the process is also to have a level of understanding that you are taking the necessary steps to creating an abundant foundation for yourself. Quitting your job with zero savings in your bank when you haven't even started your agency, your content creation platform, or your product line isn't taking a risk—it's being foolish.

The industry you are in will most likely determine the speed at which revenue will start to trickle—or pour!—in. For example, I have been podcasting for about two and a half years, and we are just now starting to make money. With my agency, however, I was making a full time salary by month three. I would never have quit my job or deserted an income stream for my podcast from day one. It would have put immense financial strain on my shoulders and on the breathing life of Okay Sis, a pressure it shouldn't bear as it is growing itself, a pressure that would have crippled it. When I started working on my agency, I was also working a full-time job. I quit that full-time job four months into starting Scout's Agency, which as my dad said to me was way too soon but I said before, I jump without checking if my parachute is locked and loaded. I am never *too* calculated but I wait for proof of concept before making large decisions.

Conversations to have and questions to ask before quitting your day job to pursue your business full time:

- What do I need on a monthly basis to pay my bills and support my basic needs?
- How much do I have in savings and how many months will my savings support me if I can't take a full monthly salary out of my business?
- What expenses can I cut back on for the next few months while I give my business the room to breathe and grow?
- If I have a partner, have I communicated with them my plan and are they supportive of the realities of the risk I am taking?
- If I have a family, are their basic needs (housing, education, food, medical) going to be able to be met as I pursue my business full time?
- If I do need to cut back on some of our basic needs, what am I willing to cut back on? Think: a new apartment at a lower rent cost, a lower car payment, or cooking dinner at home instead of ordering take-out every night.
- Do I feel good about the proof of concept that my business is currently exhibiting for me to take it to the next level?
- Do I believe in myself? Do I believe that this is what I am destined for? Do I believe that I got this? Do I believe that I deserve this new life?

So, take a look at your financial situation and be realistic about your business revenue projections but also add in some magic. Over planning can strangle the energy of your new venture but having a level of responsibility can give your new venture the right womb in which to grow in.

But that is just financial risk. There is also emotional risk. When you go out on your own to follow what your solar plexus chakra is begging you to do, you risk the fact that your closest ones to you will feel anxious for you, you risk putting yourself out there for others to formulate their own public opinion about you, or you risk stepping into the world with your bare soul. You'll find that all of those things will bring you closer to yourself than you have ever been before. You will shed the expectations of others so quickly that the only person you will report to is yourself.

In order to manage all this financial and emotional risk, we must first label it. Being able to identify out loud which risks we are and are not taking, and then finding suitable tools to help ease the uncertainty can make the difference between an entrepreneur on auto-pilot and an entrepreneur that acts with intention.

Turn inwards before answering these journal prompts so that you can not only accurately identify the biggest risk that is weighing on your heart, but also so that you can accurately pick the tool that will help you face risk with clarity.

The Risk Intake Form:

What is the main financial risk I am taking with starting my business?

_____

_____

_____

What is one way I can off-set that financial risk today by either saving elsewhere or managing my money differently?

_____

_____

_____

In what ways is taking this financial risk making me stronger?

_____

_____

_____

What is the main emotional risk I am taking with starting my business?

_____

_____

_____

What is one self-care tool I can implement into my daily routine to offset that emotional risk?

_____

_____

_____

In what ways is taking this emotional risk making me stronger?

_____

_____

_____

What am I slated to gain if I take these risks? What future am I building?

_____

_____

_____

When it comes to taking risks myself, I find the entire process to be quite exhilarating but also prompts quite a lot of emotional instability. In order to offset that emotional instability, I have to practice grounding techniques and rituals in order to bring myself back to my foundation.

Here are my go-to grounding rituals I love and swear by:

Grounding: Literally called grounding, I try to get this one in every day. Grounding is when you take your shoes off and walk on the dirt, grass, sand, or piece of Earth barefoot. This direct connection with the Earth has therapeutic benefits over mood. Add in deep inhales and exhales and this moment will ground you to the bigger picture: Mother Earth.

Meditation: Meditation or the act of simply just getting quiet and being with yourself sans distractions can be extremely helpful for discovering the root core of yourself. I find that when things get frantic or I am taking on more uncertainty, spending at least five minutes a day slowing down, putting my phone away, closing my eyes and simply breathing allows me to connect to the inner core of who I am.

Essential Oils: I have the Balanced blend by DoTerra which is excellent for grounding. I put it on my ankles, the bottoms of my feet, and my wrists before taking three deep breaths. This small ritual accompanied by the scent of the essential oil will remind you to ground inward.

Move Your Body Intuitively: Whenever I am feeling as if I am living in the land of risk, I intuitively tap into my body and move it in the way it is begging me to move it. Sometimes that is getting into downward facing dog, going through a sun salutation, or resting into child's pose. Other times, it is dancing expressively since no one is watching me and other times, it is moving my body in slow movements that are not based on technique. Dropping into the body and feeling into your muscles is a beautiful way to release some of the chaotic energy of the mind when you are taking on more risk.

Put Your Phone Away 1 Hour Before Bed: When you are taking on more risk with your business, your mind is going to stir up a storm. Make sure that bedtime is sacred because getting in quality sleep is going to ensure the strength of your mental health which will then ensure the strength of your work performance the next day. My favorite way to turn the brain off before bed is to put my phone away an hour before I want to go to sleep. Without the stimulation of text notifications and the temptation to check your email, you can enter into a more relaxing mode. Double points if you read a book before bed. That will definitely help you get a grounded and rested sleep.

I know. The entire thing seems risky—financially, emotionally—but the fruit on the other end is sweeter than anything your taste buds have danced with. When you make a deal with risk, you also make a deal with magic. When you make a deal with risk, you also make a deal that your reality can be anything you want it to be. You become the hand of the poet in an increasingly epic and romantic stanza.

The Lesson: Risk is the ticket into the concert - and believe me, the music will move you.

THE MOMENT YOU
STOP BLAMING
YOUR LIFE'S
CIRCUMSTANCES ON
EXTERNAL FACTORS
IS THE MOMENT YOU
START MOLDING
A FUTURE THAT IS
ALIGNED WITH YOUR
TRUE DESIRES.

Lesson #9:

Sometimes You Have To Set A Higher Standard

"Not every opportunity is a good opportunity, don't be afraid to say no."

-Dom Roberts, Podcaster

There is one affirmation, one statement, one sad settling phrase that sinks my heart and simultaneously drives my mind up a gear or two when I hear it uttered out of a fellow woman's mouth; *"It's good for now."* A swelling pressure starts swirling in my chest and my reaction is always a visceral one—my body cannot take watching another human being settling for something that is good for now. And then, I word vomit and cling onto any attempt to infuse this person with inspiration to take control of their lives and make every external situation that decorates their life to be colorful, vibrant, and soulful.

We live up to the expectations we set for ourselves. We skate within the standards that we believe our life is confined within. These invisible cages of ceilings are the reason everything in your life is the way it currently is: your job, your apartment, your closet, your savings, your relationship, your morning and night routine. To transcend beyond the state of living you are currently in and curate an even more extraordinary level of existence, you have to set a higher standard for your life. And setting a higher standard for your life means shattering the ceiling you thought was possible for someone like you.

Whether you are an immigrant, a survivor of the foster system, a kid that went to private school their whole lives, a member of the LGBTQ+ community, a cancer survivor, a woman entering adulthood and is scared shitless—you can create a higher standard for your life. It doesn't matter if you came from money or if you came from scarcity, what matters is the level at which you believe you can play at. That level is entirely made up in your mind, yet we like to believe external circumstances predestined it for us. Adversaries and hardship whether they are institutional, health-based, or fostered in our childhood are very real factors in our life. They are also not the defining judge for our future. They may be where we started but they have zero say in where you end up. In fact, if you use those adversaries as your superpower, your true standard knows no limits.

I went to a Jewish day school my entire life and still harbor within me such beautiful memories of community and safety. I have always dreamed of recreating that experience for my future children—giving them a community which was supportive, loving, and tight knit. One day, I went to check out how much that exact day school cost per year. My jaw nearly dropped: $25,000 for *kindergarten*. Thoughts started swirling in my mind; *How will I ever be able to afford that? And even if I could afford that for one of my kids, I wanted more than one and now that is just too much.* That price tag did not fit within the standard of my life in that current moment. I filed away sending my kids to the same private school I went to as a reality that was not in my scope. I put my phone away and settled for something other than the vision I had in my heart.

The same year I had that belief, I also invested over $17,000 in myself with a mindset coach and a guide to walk me through the book writing process. If I had $17,000 to invest in myself without thinking twice or disrupting my current lifestyle, and with the belief and notion that I will continue growing financially every single year, then making a $25,000 private school payment if I so choose to send my children there is possible. That is now possible for me. By investing in that high-ticket price point for coaching and guides, I was financially expanded. With this new standard, I am now putting money away to meet that tuition so that when the time comes, I will be able to do it without straining our family's finances. I will be able to do it lovingly and abundantly. This new standard put the wheels in motion for me to play on that plane. These things are now possible for me.

Let's talk about what that looks like in business. If your standard is to make $50,000 a year, that is what you will strive for. If you don't believe six-figure incomes are in your future, then they won't be because nothing can exist that is incongruent with a rooted limited belief. Your standard is what you aspire to and with that aspiration comes consistent baby steps that levels you up every single day. When you stop blaming your life's circumstances on external factors is the moment you start molding a future that is aligned with your true desires.

I used to blame my life's circumstances (my bipolar disorder) as the reason my life was stagnant and repressed, regardless of growing up in a beautiful and privileged childhood.

My father immigrated to America when he was a young boy from Egypt. As my grandmother learned English and American customs, my father grew up working for his success to achieve a higher standard for himself in America. He worked three jobs to put himself through UC Berkeley. He started a company which went bankrupt and ended up in rehab before he created the business that would give him a beautiful life. That higher standard of starting his second business allowed him to work early mornings so that he could be with my sister and I when we got home from school. His business supported us, my private school education, sleepaway camps, trips to Europe over summer, my mom staying home to take care of us, and a comfortable and abundant lifestyle. But most importantly, it supported me with the ability to go after my own dreams.

Unfortunately, within that financial privilege that my dad worked so hard to create for me, the privilege of my mental health began deteriorating rapidly. With the severe symptoms I was experiencing that left me completely out of touch with the control I had over my own life, I stayed stagnant because I repeatedly blamed the deck of cards I was dealt with—voices in my head telling me to kill myself, going paralyzed for hours because my nervous system was so fried, drowning in depression, and being monitored by therapists and doctors. It was my evidence that I could not rise higher, own my own business, be financially independent, or create the life of my dreams. I often felt guilty that what my dad had worked so hard to create was not the guarantee of a happy, fulfilling life. That even with financial safety, I was still mentally ill.

It would have been easy for me to chalk up my entire future to living with a severe mental illness which doctors were constantly monitoring. It would have been easy for me to point to my past mental states and predict a similar future. It would have been easy for me to not see the power I had to swiftly change things around.

Finally, I stared at myself in the mirror. Tears were streaming down my face as Frank Sinatra's My Way was playing on repeat in the background. Here I was, spending a weekend alone at The Parker in Palm Springs with my phone and laptop in my car so that I could finish writing this book. Here I was, after years of not knowing if I could hold a job I was creating one of my own that has made me more money than I ever expected for myself at the age of twenty-nine. Here I was, dreaming of my future and setting an even higher standard for the me I get to meet in five, ten, even twenty years. I sang the words out loud: I did it my way.

In that moment, locking eyes with myself and crying a heavy flow of tears, I thanked twenty-one year old Scout for setting a higher standard for herself that night at her mother's house, talking to her then-boyfriend, now-husband about his boundaries on being with me if I were to not take care of myself. I thanked her for choosing her.

And now, I am asking you to choose you.

You might come from poverty, be the first to graduate college, be a survivor of sexual abuse, found yourself in a verbally or physically abusive relationship, lived through health issues that compromised your future wellbeing, watched your parents get divorced, had to be the support system to a loved one with addiction problems, manage ADHD in the academic system, experienced the most gut-wrenching break up that left you lost, experienced rejection over and over and over again professionally or personally, lived through homelessness, or was told that your wildest dream was not possible and to table it for a different life time.

Whatever your story is, wherever it lies in the large breadth of human experiences, I am asking you to thank your past so that in this moment you can choose you.

Because when you choose you, you set a new standard for your life.

If you're here with me, let's talk about how to set that new standard. When setting a new higher standard it is important to be realistic. Your subconscious won't immediately believe that you can go from making minimum wage to having a multiple six-figure income in one year. While that totally can happen because I believe in miracles, the connection to action might not match up with that intense of a level up. It's like wanting to run 10 miles. You can have that as an ultimate goal, as the umbrella for your dreams, but today you start with running one. Identify what the next standard for your life is that you want to live within. It can be hiring support for your business or it can be matching your day job income so that you can go full time on your own thing.

Let's set your higher standard.

What is the financial standard you are living in today?

_____

_____

_____

What is one thing you do not want to stand for anymore that lives within the standard you are currently living out?

_____

_____

_____

What is the next higher standard from the one you are currently living today that feels doable but also expansive?

_____

_____

_____

What is the next higher standard from that one and what does it look like for your future life?

_____

_____

_____

Do you commit to holding the vision of that higher standard for yourself? And if so, in what ways are you going to commit to it?

_____

_____

_____

Coming to the realization that the ornaments that make up your life are all a reaction to the standard you self-imposed is incredibly freeing. If you created all of this by subscribing to the initial standard you were born into, imagine what you can create with a new one. Your business is a fragment of your entire reality. Set that high standard for that fragment as you will find that your business will move forward the images you dream of in your head and bring them to form in your outer reality.

The Lesson: Never settle for "good for now." You deserve more.

THE CHOICES YOU MAKE SHAPE THE REALITY YOU LIVE IN.

Lesson #10:

You Always Have Two Choices

"We are never powerless, we all have the ability to tap into our power by examining the choices that we have available to us. Every choice won't be easy, but when we exercise our ability to choose, we also learn that we have the power to do hard things."

-Minaa B. Writer, Wellness Coach, Therapist

It was a Thursday morning, and I remember being visited by a hint of my old friend depression. It was creeping up my esophagus, tightening the vibrancy of my heart's pulsation, and restricting a peaceful flow of thoughts within my mind. The feelings were just in the warning sign phase, and so I began to ponder how they would unfold and the level they would take my day over with. Slight panic started to overthrow my nervous system as I was afraid of the emotion that had the potential to take over the driver's seat.

I stepped into the shower and let the hot water trickle from my skull down to my cracked heels, allowing the steam to open my pores and soften my anxiety. As my eyes closed and I sat within the blackness of my inner eyelids, a simple command came through my third eye. It said, *"You have two choices here. To allow the depression to take over or to implement your tools in order to nurture and soothe it."*

The simplicity of the message struck me profoundly: you have two choices.

I opened my eyes vividly to see the tiles of my shower wall, yes, but also to see a basic yet powerful decision making tool that would steer me towards having each next decision and action I take fuel my highest alignment.

Everything in our life comes down to two choices: to do or not to do. It can be applied to the way we take care of our bodies to the way we do business. Boiling down our day-to-day decisions within the framework of two choices empowers us to skip over overwhelm and exercise certainty and clarity. It allows us to see the bigger picture and larger scope at hand without drowning ourselves within the subtleties and nuances of emotional responses, potential details, and future tripping.

For example, you have two choices when it comes to: starting your side hustle, signing a client, launching a third product, hiring an employee, posting consecutively to Instagram, employing mindset tools when responding to an angry email, or bringing on a business partner.

You can do all of those things. Or you cannot. You have two simple and direct choices.

Many times in entrepreneurship, people get bogged down with decisions and the gravity each tiny decision can make on the future health of their business. We can get stuck in the "what ifs" of the process or get lost in the different future branches our brand can develop into. Making decisions can feel important and heavy and that is because they are. They can entice delving into a total market research, customer feedback data analysis, gathering the opinions of others, and mapping out pros and cons lists. And while all of this can be vital in making an informed decision, there comes a point where it is also crucial to make that decision and then move on with confidence in your choices. Within the research and the feedback can come confusion which is why boiling down the scenario to two choices - to do it or not to do it—simplifies and deescalates the pressure of the decision.

If the decision is a multiple part, more complex offering or feels too large to oversimplify, you can still boil down each step to the two choices in order to chip away toward your final decision.

Let's look at the example of, *Should I create a workshop as a separate revenue model for my business?* This is a real life example that I put this method to the test with as I created Scout's Agency first workshop, *Get Yourself as a Guest on Podcasts.*

When the idea of starting a workshop popped into my mind, the oversimplification of this business decision could be boiled down to: do I do it or do I not do it? But I needed more details. I needed to feel into the process to see if I actually did want to do it. So, I mapped out three top action and execution items that would be necessary to implement the workshop.

1. Film video modules of me explaining the material to guide our students through
2. A PDF worksheet that is custom designed that those who are leading themselves through the workshop can utilize to maximize results
3. Hiring a FB ads manager to help promote the workshop

These are three of the steps that I would have to take if I wanted to complete my original idea: Should I create a workshop as a separate revenue model for my business? I gave myself two choices for each of these three tasks: do it or don't do it. As I felt into my soul on whether or not these tasks lit me up or felt more like a responsibility or a "have-to," my answer was clear. I was excited, my heart started racing, and the creative ideas on where to film the video modules and how to present the accompanying PDF started running wild in my mind. I decided that for each of these three tasks that I would do it.

Seeing that I made the decision to take action over the micro decisions helped me come to the majorly clear answer on if I should start the workshop. The answer was yes and today, it exists for all women who are looking to become a guest on podcasts and aren't in a position to pay a monthly retainer for our services. We created the workshop and have watched women guide themselves through Scout's Agency's methodology and best practices for getting our clients as guests on podcasts to successfully land themselves as a guest to tell their stories. (If you are interested in this workshop, head on over to www.scoutsagency.com to sign up!)

That wouldn't have become a reality however had those three micro tasks not have been a "do it" decision. Sometimes the big decision seems like a "do it" but when you break it into the micro tasks, you find a different answer. This happened to me when

I was considering merging my agency with another agency. The big picture was telling me to do it but as I broke it down into micro-actions that saying yes to the big picture decision of merging my agency with another would entail, I realized that those micro-actions weren't in alignment. I said I didn't want to do it for each of them. What at first glance seemed like an exciting, aligned idea that I was ready to jump into then spun a different story as I put three micro actions that would come with that decision to the two choices test.

I simplified the big decision with three micro-decisions that would come with supporting the big decision and asked myself without wavering into vague terror: *Do I want to do this or do I not want to do this?*

Understanding that you have two choices with everything in your business is also extremely empowering. Suddenly, the choices you make shape the reality you live in. If you choose to work primarily with female-founded brands (like me!), that starts shaping the ethos of your brand. If you choose not to bring on a business partner, that develops you as the main leader of the ship. If you choose to not have an Instagram and be a word-of-mouth-only business, that places you in a unique marketing advantage. If you choose to create an accessible workshop around your expertise, you create a new space to put your energy towards. But when the decisions feel endless and the future avenues debilitating, pause your workflow and ask yourself, "Do I want to do this, or do I not want to do this?" The clarity will rise within your chest, and your soul will scream the right answer to you if you have the foresight to get quiet and listen. Then, you get to proceed with that aligned vision.

Narrowing your life down to two decisions seems like an over simplification or even too easy of a solution, but do know that I am known to be quite blunt with this philosophy.

My sister and I have very different working styles when it comes to Okay Sis Podcast. Mady likes to perfect things like font style, graphic design, and branding. I like to look at a few fonts, pick the one that feels the best to me, and move on to the next decision. There is beauty in both styles and downfalls to both. I perhaps oversimplify my decisions while my sister perhaps overcomplicates them. Many times, we will be having a repetitive conversation about something we haven't pulled the trigger on when my patience runs out and I hastily blurt out, "Are we doing this or not?" There is a bluntness to it which catches my sister off guard (I am working on my delivery) but it is in that moment when that question is posed that we actually make a decision and move towards other progress in the business. The blockage is released and the current of creation is opened.

The idea of having two choices can also end the idea phase once and for all. I hear the same thing constantly from so many of my friends. They want to start their own thing, they want to launch a YouTube channel, they want to write a cookbook. I listen to the same narrative six months later as they let me know they just haven't decided what to call the book or which camera to use to shoot their vlogs or which website provider to go with. When I reach a breaking point of indulging in their broken record-ness, I simply ask, "Are you going to do it or not?"

If it is a no, they aren't distracting themselves with a potential idea that will never come to fruition allowing them space to focus on the things that truly will propel their lives forward. If it is a yes, they will get the idea out of their mind and into the physical world getting them one step closer to their dream goals.

Turn inward and think about the one area of your life or in your business that you are avoiding making a decision over. Let's put it to the two choices test.

What is the decision you are trying to make:

What are three micro-actions that you will have to take if you decide to say yes to that decision? Once you list them, fill out the column to the right on whether or not you want to take those actions or see those tasks through. Have it be a gut reaction! No need to overthink. Your intuition knows the answer.

1. _____ *Do I want to do it?* Y | N
2. _____ *Do I want to do it?* Y | N
3. _____ *Do I want to do it?* Y | N

Based on the answers to your three micro-actions, take it back to the big decision you are trying to make. You have two choices. Are you going to do it or are you not going to do it?

How does the clarity and declaration of that decision make you feel?

Always keep in mind that there is no right answer, but the answer will move energy. For example, my sister came to me with a big business idea that she wanted to execute with me. I wanted to do the big business idea but one of the micro-actions would have been to take outside investment. I don't want to take on outside investment. That type of business doesn't jam with the type of lifestyle or the type of entrepreneur I want to be. Since one of the main micro-actions was a no, the big decision was also a no. It wasn't a wrong decision, it was just the decision that works best for my energy and for the vision of my future.

Our minds are complicated spaces to dwell in. They catastrophize, ruminate, or exaggerate. They keep us in the thinking phase with fear. They overcomplicate the decisions of our lives.

Break that cycle with simplicity and bluntness: are you going to do this or not?

The Lesson: Anchor yourself with the power of two choices when you feel overwhelmed.

ONCE YOU
SURRENDER TO
ABUNDANCE, THE
UNIVERSE WILL
START THROWING
SYNCHRONICITIES
AT YOU THAT
WILL OPEN THE
POSSIBILITY TO
MONEY MIRACLES.

Lesson # 11:

Lack Mindset Is A Waste Of Time

"When you let go of frantic and pushy energy, you start to get your creativity back. Believe that you deserve good things, and watch your luck change."

-Jaci Marie, co-host of What We Said Podcast

I remember the unsettling anxiety looking at my revenue during those months. It was dismal and not going to make ends meet and I was starting to panic. I would bounce back and forth between my business account and my personal savings account, which was dwindling because out of a complete denial and potential naiveté, I did not scale back my monthly spending regardless of the fact that my monthly revenue could barely cover my salary. I was scrambling for clients while simultaneously avoiding sales emails because by month three of this chaos, I was strengthening that limiting belief within that told me signing clients and having a consistent income within my business was impossible. And it was out of that belief that I was acting, reacting, and creating.

I don't remember the aha moment where I learned about the difference between lack mindset versus abundance mindset but I do know where that teaching first permeated my subconscious. I was in a spiritual mastermind with women who were in their first six months of business. We met every other week, had virtual lectures from other women in business, and had an ongoing group chat where we celebrated wins and looked to one another for advice. We did a lot of emotional, energetic, and spiritual mindset work around money—our relationship to it, our perceptions of it, our limiting beliefs around what we can and cannot have in this lifetime. After doing deep work around my money boundaries and taking the much needed hard look at my finances, I surrendered to the fact that I would have to work with my money and not against it.

I decided to cultivate an abundance mindset and act out of that intention versus a space of lack and anxiety. I started believing (and just seeing the truth of the matter) that there were endless clients that were not only available to work with me but wanted to work with me. I started believing that I deserve a flowing stream of money coming in and that the parameters on my monthly revenue goals could expand significantly. I started believing that I was worthy of money, that she would want to come into my space, and that if I trusted that the flow of my clients was the exact flow that was needed for me in that moment, that I would surrender the panic to something greater. Within that surrender, my energy would be expansive and people would want to work with me.

And they did.

I doubled my revenue that next month and continued to grow month and month and month after that—in 2020 nonetheless, amidst economic turbulent times due to the pandemic. I ended 2020 having grown 250% from 2019, our first year in business.

This is not to say that I sat on a pillow, cultivated these beliefs with my eyes closed focusing on my breath, and opened my laptop to ten clients saying they wanted to sign with me. I always like to remind myself and others that within mindset and manifestation work comes the responsibility to co-create with the universe. If you don't show up, the results will be lost. However, once you surrender to abundance, the universe will start throwing synchronicities at you that will open the possibility to money miracles. When you make decisions to show up, the results of showing up are energetically attracted to you.

When I signed a three-month contract to work with my mindset coach one-on-one, I was in replenishing mode of my roster. Playing with the idea of making the biggest personal investment in myself with her was contrasted against the thoughts of, *I need to sign a few more clients first.* After going through my fears with her, I decided to open myself to the universe through my abundant mindset. I energetically made the decision to invest in myself, which would allow me to show up in a greater way in my business to attract higher paying clients. I energetically made a contract with the universe: I'll show up if you will.

I signed a three-month contract to work with Amy Natalie, who is still my coach today, and put down the most money I had ever invested in myself. The next day, I signed two clients putting my roster at its all time highest.

The magic in an abundant mindset—and any expansive, positive, and healthy mindset—can be dwindled down to the ripple effect these mindsets can have on happenings in your business and the action you take after circumstances unfold.

Take this example. The same three things happen to two different people in one day: their Instagram account gained 100 followers, a client broke their contract, and a sales call went well with a dream potential client.

The individual with the lack mindset will see these circumstances as a loss revenue stream that needs to be replenished as soon as possible. In this perceived emergency energy, she reaches out to potential clients that are not aligned and not a fit for the longevity of her brand or her passion in hopes of getting that revenue number back up immediately. She fails to engage with her new social media audience—where aligned clients may be living— because she is so focused on how to get back the money she has lost. With that energy, she tries to seal the deal with that dream client she had a sales call with by suffocating their space to make a decision with numerous follow-ups. In return, they do not sign.

The individual with the abundant mindset will see the opportunity and the growth: an increase in their community on social media and the prospect of working with a dream client —both expansive offerings that are creating more positive space in the business as a client is stepping down. This individual trusts that one client leaving is opening up space for a potentially more aligned client and a more engaged community. She is excited at the growth and is at peace with the broken contract. Within this space, she is ready to land her dream client and engage with her new followers from a place of gratitude and passion. Through this energy, she signs the dream client and has three prospective sales emails waiting in her inbox.

The individual with the abundant mindset has better chances of signing that dream client and turning her new community members into potential revenue streams in the future than the one with the lack mindset. Regardless of the identical events happening to both women, they will each take drastically different courses of action dependent on if they are operating from a lack mindset or an abundant mindset.

If this doesn't quite resonate, ask yourself this: Would you feel good about buying a product from someone whose energy is anxious, scrambling, and desperate? Or would you rather buy a similar product from someone who is confident, secure, and grateful?

Identifying a lack mindset starts with diving into your relationship with money, which if I am being honest, is a continuous journey that I always have to drop into. The households we were raised in and the belief systems around money that our parents hold true are often passed down or at the very least etched into our subconscious. In childhood, we learn from the source: our family. If our parents were reckless with money, never had enough of it, worked too hard to get it therefore they did not have the time to spend with us, or garnered constant anxiety around keeping it, those belief systems will shape the way we view the flow of our bank accounts today.

A lack mindset around money can manifest itself through the following beliefs:

> *Only those that were born into money have a chance at making it.*
> *Making money is hard and in order to really make it big, you have to slave your life away.*
> *Money never sticks around. It comes into my bank account as fast as it goes.*

I always have to find a deal or a sale because money is never guaranteed for me.
Money is evil and if I ask for it while making a sale, I am greedy.
There is a finite amount of resources when it comes to money, and I am not someone it gets to visit often.
Money comes easily to other people but not to me.

If any of those ring a bell, then it's time to identify where your lack mindset around money is coming from. Was it something your father said to you as a little girl? Was it watching your mother sneak in the back door with shopping bags telling you to not tell dad? Was it feeling guilty for buying anything that wasn't a necessity? Was it watching your parents work three jobs to barely make ends meet? Was it the lectures your dad gave you that the reason you have all of this is because he worked hard and was strict about his money management?

It took me a very long time to realize that the beliefs and practices around money that my mother and my father have (which are both quite different) are not the holy scripture. Their ways of managing money do not need to be the way I navigate my relationship with money.

I do not choose to see money as finite that only some of us are destined to have. I do not choose to see money as this rare commodity that if found is because we merely hit the jackpot. I do not choose to see money as a metric unit that only me or my competitor get to have - we both get to have it. I do not choose to see money as something that is hard to obtain. I do not choose to see money as the dictator over the quality of my life.

I see money as an easy energetic flow and dance that I get to be a part of. I choose to see it through the lens of endless possibilities and creative opportunities. I believe in my heart that there is an abundant well of clients I can serve now and in the future. I believe my services have the potential to financially soar. I believe that I can receive money and not need to be a helicopter parent with it. I believe I can give away money, not control it so tightly, and indulge with my money and that it will still be available for me if I show up to receive it. I trust that money wants to find me because I respect and love her, without the need to control her.

I found myself, almost a year later in the exact same position I was in with my mindset coach. She invited me to be a part of her upcoming mastermind of female entrepreneurs and the monthly ticket price was higher than what I was currently paying her. She invited me into the mastermind knowing that due to COVID economic complications, I had two big clients that were unable to continue working with me after their contract was up (even though we both still wanted to keep going!). I told her it wasn't the best timing to ask me to pay more monthly for an upgraded service as I was in sales mode to replenish. She looked at me and reminded me of who I am and what I believe. She said, *"I have seen you sign two big clients in one week. Do you really believe you won't sign another client within the next month?"*

I smiled at her. No, I didn't believe I wouldn't. I knew I would. I knew that my rational fear-based mind was showing up to the conversation. I looked at her and said, *"Let's do it. Sign me up."*

I signed four clients within the next two weeks. Because I believed. Because I showed up. Because I knew that money is available if I show up and serve those I need to serve.

Say this real quick out loud: Money is and will always be available to me.

How did that feel? Expansive? Exciting? Enriching?

What if you took that sentiment and belief system into a sales call instead of one that is anxious and in need of controlling the out come out of a belief that if every sale does not come your way, you will be in a state of lack?

If you're unsure of the answer, I have it for you: miracles will happen.

The moment you choose to see the expansive opportunities in your business and within your revenue stream while meeting others from a place of trust, confidence, and excitement is when opportunities begin rolling in. The universe supports the energy you exude. If your energy is restrictive and chaotic, your results will parallel a similar frequency. If your energy is abundant and open, you will see the external factors of your business as an open invitation to walk through yet another door towards opportunities and total success.

The Lesson: Your mindset can change the trajectory of how you tap into potential revenue streams and the successes of your business.

AS THE PROJECTOR, YOU HOLD THE POWER OF THE IMAGE AND THE NARRATIVE YOU SO DEEPLY DESIRE. YOUR BUSINESS WILL ONLY GROW AS LARGE AS YOUR BELIEF IN IT.

Lesson #12:

Limiting Beliefs Rule Your World

"Shine a light on your subconscious limiting beliefs, see them with compassion, and watch as they start to dissolve. Create space to plant seeds for new beliefs that will blossom into your upgraded reality."

-Amy Natalie, Intuitive Mindset Coach

My husband scored a projector and projecting screen for free on Craigslist. When we lived in our mid-century modern apartment with concrete walls and concrete ceilings and concrete pillars interrupting rooms, we would invite friends over and he would set it up on the communal rooftop. We took the cushions from the outdoor sofas that huddled around the fire pit and created an outdoor movie theater. Friends brought wine, others bought chips to snack on. We spent the night beneath the stars at our makeshift theater as the images and sounds of the film shot out from the projector and splashed itself onto the white cloth screen for us all to get lost within.

I like to think of myself as a projector and the screen as my business. The images that swirl around me will be projected as the story that my business tells. People will huddle around to watch that movie (my clients) and others will be in the movie (my team). And it starts with what I dream in my head and eventually, after I have extracted the idea out of my mind, what I put out there into the world.

But the images and the dreams and the ideas of your mind's ability to make it out of those confines and project itself onto a dazzling oversized white screen depend on one fundamental factor: your limiting beliefs.

What is a limiting belief? A limiting belief is a false and oftentimes deeply rooted belief that keeps you from achieving or reaching a goal. It hinders your ability to properly execute. It chars away at your confidence. It keeps you playing small. It blocks off the expansive possibility of your success by placing parameters around your potential. It justifies reasons why you won't go out of your comfort zone. It kills the dream before you write your strategy to achieve it. It is your succeeding threshold.

What do limiting beliefs look like? They vary from person to person but here are a few examples that you might be familiar with:

I don't have anything to bring to the table.
I can't increase my prices because if I do, I will lose my clients.
I can't start a podcast because I don't have enough expertise to share.
My business hours have to be from 9-5 or else I won't be able to keep up with the rest of the world.
My services are not valued enough for me to turn this into a six-figure business.
People don't want to watch another YouTuber talk about makeup.
If I put myself out there, people will judge me and my reputation will be over.
If I share my personal life online, my professional life will be over.
I have to graduate from college in order to have a successful career.
I need to be a certain weight if I am going to make it as an influencer.
I have nothing unique to offer to the world.

These are all false narratives our ego tells us to keep us in our comfort zone, the land where dreams played into reality don't exist. They are also narratives we have picked up from society and have been translated in our mind as solid fact. When you think about going against a limiting belief, your heart probably starts to race because you are entering into territory that isn't on the exact map we were given as children. Fear will creep in and others will have opinions: "What do you mean you are quitting your job with benefits to open up a flower shop?" Acting in spite of a limiting belief can feel uncomfortable and risky but I believe staying in one is the ultimate betrayal to who you are, inside there, without all of these outside constructed opinions.

Let's dissect one of my limiting beliefs that I picked up from society: If I share that I live with bipolar disorder in my professional life, no one will want to work with me.

That is a pretty understandable limiting belief because after all my disorder has landed me in the hospital, stolen internships and jobs from me, and at one point wiped me right out of functioning in society. There were moments when I was unable to complete the responsibilities I agreed to take on so if I share that I live with bipolar disorder, my clients might not feel comfortable betting their money on me. We are used to as a society downplaying our health weaknesses at work—even our family life at work if we are mothers —so that we are seen as entirely competent almost robot like candidates to our bosses. The problem with this is that we are human and our humanness will illuminate itself through the cracks one way or another.

So yes, this limiting belief is rooted in some fact: people with mental illness for a very long time were not open about their mental health in the workplace nor would they openly say as the CEO or the founder of a company that they lived with depression, anxiety, psychosis, mood swings, catatonia, or were on a plethora of psychiatric drugs.

But that doesn't mean that no one will want to work with me if I share my mental illness with them. In fact, I quickly realized the truth was the exact opposite.

I started sharing my story of living with bipolar disorder on podcasts. My sister and I were a guest on Chatty Broads with Bekah Martinez and Jess Ambrose. The four of us got together to record an episode all around mental illness and it is there that I told my story on a very large public platform. I was a few months into running Scout's Agency at the time.

What happened was an onslaught of women reaching out who were experiencing the same thing, or had a significant other or friend who was suffering from a mental illness. People started

DMing me for advice and I started sharing mental health content on my Instagram, which is very much public and available to follow for all of my clients.

And then, as my identity on Okay Sis Podcast and my personal Instagram was very rooted in the notion that I suffered from bipolar disorder but that I was also very, incredibly open about living with a mental illness, I started to open that door at work.

It was a slow build. I started, in appropriate conversations with clients I had come close to, mentioning that I suffer from a mental illness. As clients started following my Instagram account, they started figuring it out for themselves. In the beginning, I was nervous. No, petrified. Would I lose them as clients? Would they see me as less competent to run their account? Would they not trust that I was as dependable as they thought? Was my limiting belief about to come true?

And, gloriously, the opposite happened. My relationships with my clients deepened every time they uncovered my story with bipolar disorder. They respected me more. They championed behind me to an even greater extent. They loved the perseverance in my human story.

I shared my story of living with bipolar and everyone still wanted to work with me. In fact, they wanted to work with me more.

Limiting beliefs have a way of playing sneaky tricks on your brain. They present themselves as fact. When they do, you get the opportunity to challenge them. Ask yourself, *"Is this a fact? Or is this my ego trying to tell me I am exiting my comfort zone?"* If you can identify your limiting beliefs and then imagine a scenario, or better yet find a real life living example to prove to your brain the opposite does exist, you can act according to your truth. Not your ego's truth or society's truth, but yours.

Let's start to identify these intruders to our dreams right here and break it down in three steps.

Step #1: Close your eyes and settle into your solar plexus, the nerve center (also known as the third chakra) that lies above your belly button and below your breast bone. Breathe into a narrative you tell yourself that is impeding on the success of your business. You will come across self-doubt during this process and questions like, "I really think that one is just true. There is no way I can make a quarter of a million dollars with my business." Challenge yourself to challenge these beliefs. The more resistance you feel to a belief, the more evidence that we are dealing with a limiting one.

Step #2: Let's identify them on paper, negate them, and then act despite them. Utilize the limiting belief worksheet on the following page to help guide you. Write down the limiting belief that came to you when you connected to your solar plexus. Now that we know the ceilings we are working with, let's rewrite this limiting belief negating its cage. As you write down your new belief, know that you don't have to believe it right now. You don't have to believe it overnight. In fact, tearing down limiting beliefs takes evidence and opposite action over consistent time. We have identified them— and that is a noble first step.

But let's go a bit deeper here.

Step #3: Third step is to list out some action items of ways you can act despite the narrative you tell yourself.

Step #4: And then the last step is to identify someone who has acted out of your new belief to show your brain evidence that something like this is possible in this lifetime.

Here is my limiting belief breakdown for you to resort back to in case you get stuck during this clarity exercise.

My top limiting belief: If I share that I live with bipolar disorder in my professional life, no one will want to work with me.

My new belief: Sharing my journey with bipolar disorder in healthy ways will humanize me, allowing me to get closer to my clients and usher in the individuals that I am destined to work with on a connection level. I can share who I am in the workplace and still be successful. In fact, that is my superpower around success.

One action I can take: I will record a podcast episode talking about my favorite healing tools I have picked up because of my bipolar disorder and publish it.

My evidence: Steve Jobs suffered from a mental illness and he was still widely respected and revered.

Your turn to expand!

My top limiting belief: _____

My new belief: _____

One action I can take: _____

My evidence: _____

Always know that as the projector, you hold the power of the image and the narrative you so deeply desire. Your business will only grow as large as your belief in it is. And if that belief is limited, your success, your growth, and your place as a leader in your space will be limited as well. Challenge your beliefs around your potential, and your potential will expand. Your business will take its place, standing proudly in the land of entrepreneurship.

The Lesson: Limiting beliefs keep you playing small, but once you identify them, you get to determine the new belief system that will oil your machine to run beautifully.

YOU CAN WORK
FROM A PLACE OF
CALM, FROM A PLACE
OF SERENITY, FROM
A PLACE OF PASSION
AND INTEGRITY AND
INTENTION AND
YOUR BUSINESS WILL
GROW.

Lesson # 13:

How You Show Up Is What You Get Back In Return

"You get to decide. You get to decide on what to call in. On who you work with. On what you get paid. Your energy is your currency - you spend it and share it with whom you decide. That is your power."

-Whitney Eckis, Founder of Eckis Marketing
& CEO of Get Supr

I was sitting in a pool of sweat on the verge of tears with welling anxiety building within my gut. I was working with a woman where I could feel her wall of expectations grow brick by brick by brick. Every time she emailed me or I received an email regarding her account, my heart froze if the news wasn't favorable. I was taking on the aspects of our business exchange that were not in my control. I was going beyond my scope, and it didn't feel good for me. Yet, she kept asking more and more and more of me, disregarding personal boundaries or the growing hours I was working.

I remember putting it all on her: *She is disrespecting my boundaries, she is causing me all of this anxiety, she is demanding things of me I cannot create.*

And while, yes, that is partially true, the real truth lies in the matter that I created space for her to treat me like that. I showed up and went beyond my scope, I showed up and emailed her back the second she emailed me on a Saturday, I showed up and held space for her to be stressed, upset, and demanding, I showed up and took the blame for other people's actions. I was the punching bag because I took the shape of one.

In business, and in life, how you show up is what you get in return. If you list out your boundaries from the get go, they will be respected. And if someone pushes them slightly, you get to stand in your power and acknowledge that breach. It will most likely not happen again. But when you are open to anything, down for the cause, want to go above and beyond to wow your client or customer or partner, that above and beyond knows no ceiling and you will start to lose your footing and your place in it all.

I used to want to please everyone. Every client that came onto my roster was an opportunity to wow them to no end. The people pleaser in me was ready, geared up, and prepared to take on crippling amounts of anxiety if it meant my client was happy at the end of the day. I came to the table with people pleasing energy so many of my clients, who were just taking my lead, relied on me as such a force of support that it went beyond the scope of what we had both agreed on—and not just business wise, but emotionally as well. I was there to please so they gave me opportunities to fulfill my self-fulfilling prophecy.

And then I realized, all at once and over time, that I needed to regroup and come to the table with a different frequency and with different boundaries. It is in that frequency—one that holds her boundaries and sticks to the scope agreed upon without feeling the need to answer emails within five seconds of receiving them—that I gain respect from my clients. The energetic exchange coming from a rooted place of what I will and will not do is more defined, balanced, and successful for both ends of the party. I do not reach burnout based on exaggerated anxiety and I do not reach the point anymore (well, sometimes it still happens but I recognize it much quicker now!) where I am no longer in alignment with the services and the workload I sold to my client.

Quick and easy ways I implement boundaries:

- In my contract, I name the hours of operations I am available to get back to my clients
- I let my clients know that my response time can be up to 24 hours even if it is 99% of the time within a few hours—this gives me the space to breathe if I have a heavy workload day and cannot live within my inbox
- I verbalize and have it written in our contracts that my agency does not guarantee any number of results, but I do provide averages from past client work
- When I do decide to do something outside of my scope, I let my client know lovingly that that is outside of the agreed upon scope but that I feel good taking that on for her this time
- I do not apologize for things outside of my control but I do acknowledge my clients' feelings

- I keep things to email and not text messaging so that my personal space isn't invaded outside of business hours

But how you show up with others in your business is just one part of the equation here. How you show up within yourself is another game changer.

I remember I would enter my days with manic energy—pumping myself up with adrenaline to be productively inspired. I went from task to task with a level of heightened heart palpitations. I was addicted to the high of crossing each task off one by one. I was addicted to a good day's work where I moved so quickly I forgot to eat. I was addicted to, in many ways, the stress of running my business. I just somehow disguised it as pumped up passion.

It took the COVID-19 pandemic for me to see that when I slowed down and came from a calmer place, the same amount got done, my business grew, and I felt more grounded with every step of the way. When I came into my day's work feeling nourished and centered, I was able to dance with my tasks in a way that felt inspiring. I could cross tasks off without revving up my nervous system, which overtime leads to burnout and a host of other physical and mental health problems. There was power in opening up my computer after having had the morning to myself to connect within. There was power in knowing that everything did not have to get done today and that being mindful with my tasks produced better quality work. My mindset going in determined the quality at which my emotions colored my days.

This energetic shift also will trickle down to your team. If you are stressed and promoting extreme multitasking and pumping results out on tight deadlines, your team will be stressed, anxious, and on high alert. If you had the option to be stressed and anxious or calm and intentional, you would pick the latter. Yet, we default to the former when we believe that is the only way to be a successful entrepreneur.

Let's shatter that notion together. You can work from a place of calm, from a place of serenity, from a place of passion and integrity and intention and your business will grow. In fact, I would challenge this idea to say that it will probably soar much quicker than if you are coming to work from a place of extreme chaos.

The web is quick and the web never lies. The energy you walk into the day with will be the energy you take away. If you see your inbox as an endless to-do list of demands you cannot keep up with, you will be working out of a place of pressure. If you see your inbox as this flowing life force that you get to engage with, you will approach your emails with enthusiasm.

Ask yourself these questions to find the energy that you want to consciously put out into your business and into your days:

If I could pick any emotions to carry me through my work day, which would I choose?

Which emotion do I experience during my work that I would like to not experience?

What is one way I can approach the day to not experience the emotion I am approaching my day with and rather shift to the dream emotion I want to carry me through my days?

You get to decide how you want to show up on a daily basis. You get to choose if you go through your to-do list with endless stress or centered gratitude. And what is most illuminating is that how you show up will pour into your customers, your clients, your investors, and your manufacturers.

The Lesson: Identify the frequency in which you want to live and work from there.

IF YOU ARE GOING
TO CREATE A
BUSINESS THAT
FULFILLS YOU AND
NOT JUST SUSTAINS
YOU, YOU GET TO
CREATE THE WORK
CULTURE, SYSTEMS,
AND FRAME YOUR
BUSINESS OCCUPIES.

Lesson #14:

You Get To Create Whatever Environment You Want

"There's no denying this great necessity in nurturing one's mind before beginning to nurture others. This philosophy has applied itself amongst many definitions, but it's especially fundamental in work environments. French philosopher Gaston Bachelard in his book 'The Poetics of Space' quotes Noël Arnaud: 'I am the space where I am.' And as simple as those words may be, there is nothing greater than acknowledging the space you inhabit as an extension of who you are. To exist in true harmony, one must be willing to mold their space as they see fit in order to fit their trajectory. Take into consideration of your own values before you find yourself watering them down for a paycheck."

-Orion Carloto, Poet & Creator

One of the main reasons I started my business was so I could have freedom in my day to day life. Freedom to me, on a soul level, is one of the most important things to feel and have. It allows me to stay creative and malleable and aligned with myself. In all of my decisions, I assess if certain avenues will advance my freedom or take away from it.

And then, I thought that I should open up an office because that is what businesses do.

I was so excited when I signed the lease—partly because it was in my dream building where I had my closest friends as neighbors, restaurants and coffee shops filled a three block radius, and I was doing it with my first employee, my best friend. It was an experience unlike any other. I remember thinking to myself the gravity of what it meant to be responsible for two leases now: my apartment and my office. My husband was scoring vintage deals on what would become our beautiful, 12 foot long office table and a pink Gainey pot to house our fiddle fig leaf tree that my dad bought me as an office warming gift. I went to IKEA, HomeGoods, and Target to get all of the things—decoration, plates, forks and knives, towels, chairs, and white board markers.

The office was storefront and we had a decal up on the outside window that said SCOUT'S AGENCY. It was grown up, it was official, and it was aesthetically up to my standards (imagine concrete floors and super high ceilings, a loft area, and floor-to-ceiling windows). I couldn't say it enough on sales calls, "Our offices are based out of Little Italy, San Diego." Friends that lived in the area rotated in and out to say hi, stop by for lunch, have a glass of wine. It was a clubhouse of sorts in many ways—until it became a real office.

As we hired interns and part-time independent contractors, the office filled up with four or five of us instead of just me and my best friend. The pull of having rent over time made me feel as if I had to show up to the office and stay the full eight hours. I wanted to set an example for my team and if I was fluid with my schedule, I feared they would be too in a work culture that was already relaxed and independent and lenient. I suddenly realized that I was working a nine-to-five in an office, that I had somewhere to be at 9-9:30 am every morning, and that it looked best if I stayed until 5:00. My office, in all of its legitimacy and excitement, was taking away the freedom my business sought out to grant me.

Suddenly my mid-day workouts or lunch with a girlfriend or my afternoon nap vanished from my schedule. My ability to start work at 10:30 if I wanted to on a random Tuesday was off the table. I started to realize that the very thing I thought I should do—open an office—was chaining me to a lifestyle I was actively working against.

The COVID-19 pandemic helped me take this inner gut feeling and turn it into a clear decision. As we retreated into our homes for quarantine, my office sat there collecting dust for months. And, business ran as usual. And, business actually soared. And, I felt as if I had my autonomy over my days back. So, I did not renew the lease to my office because it wasn't the lifestyle I wanted for my future. I was waking up to the idea that I get to make decisions in my business that serve my highest alignment. I get to recreate the rule book.

But it wasn't until months later that this realization became an engrained practice. I was sitting outside on my Acapulco black chair in my garden on a Zoom call with my mindset coach (I love taking my calls outside!). I was recounting the areas I felt stale in my business, the areas I was feeling uninspired. She simply said to me, "This is your business. You get to change it to be whatever it is you want it to be."

And that is when the message was driven home and I was able to see my business as this expansive entity that supported my life in the ways that I wanted and needed it to support me. It was not the other way around. When I felt stuck, it was an opportunity to infuse more creativity back into my day-to-day. When I felt like launching a new service or system or workshop, I had the power to do so. When I felt like taking it easy for a few months, I had the power to claim that for my life.

This is a lesson that must ring true to you too if you are going to create a business that fulfills you and not just sustains you: you get to create the work culture, systems, and frame your business occupies. You don't have to send emails that are void of emotion and highly professional. I sign all of my emails: Love, Scout (which side-note, one journalist responded to my email highly offended and creeped out that I wrote Love, Scout and told me to please never do that again but hey—I am going to keep doing me). Your team bonding doesn't have to look like workshops where you build trust skills through rock climbing followed by a lecture from a business coach. My team bonding day included lunch, mimosas, and a shopping spree on a Tuesday afternoon. Your workdays don't have to start at 9:00 am, they can start at 10:00 am (I don't take any calls before 10:00 am). You can have a team of part time employees, a team of full time employees, or a team of freelancers. You can have an office, work remotely, or gather in co-working spaces once a week. You create exactly the work environment that you want to create within and those that are attracted to that culture will be the ones who flock to be on your team.

At Scout's Agency, I have a very different approach when it comes to my employees. If one of my team members didn't sleep well the night before and by 2:00 pm they are sitting in brain fog, they simply Slack me and say, "Hey, didn't sleep well last night and I am hitting a wall— going to take a nap!" They go to doctor appointments freely and lunches with family members that are in town without the need to let me know when they will be on and off the clock. If they need to physically re-energize their body, they will leave their computer and take a power walk. If they want to take the afternoon off and would rather finish work up later in the evening, they do so. While nine-to-five is upheld 75% of the time, they are never chained to their desk during those hours. I trust they will get their work done (and they do!) and that if there are no calls on their schedule, they will organize their day the way that works the best with their biology, inspiration levels, and in-flow moments. There is never any anxiety felt on their end if they leave their computer to take a nap, go for a walk, or meet a friend for an afternoon coffee. They know their boss isn't breathing down their neck, counting the minutes they were gone. I want their days to feel free. I want them to feel self-employed.

And if they broke up with their boyfriend the night before, I definitely want to know. Presents will be delivered to their doorstep and I clear their schedule that day so that they can take it easy. Because life happens, and I never want Scout's Agency to feel like the place they have to show up to but rather the place they get to show up to. They know that their happiness, energy levels, and fulfillment is always top of mind for me.

This is the way I construct my business and it is also the way a majority of corporations do not. I know that this self-employed mentality with all of the leniency is not for everyone. I know that many potential employees would take advantage of my emotionally open work culture. That is why I only hire those in which this structure does work and in which this structure helps them soar. And when you choose the way your business runs, you will attract like-minded people to come on board and collectively work toward the bigger mission.

I urge you in the very beginning to start thinking outside of the box. Which systems are you implementing that came from your previous corporate customer service job because you don't realize things can be done a different way? What does your dream structure look like on a daily basis? Is it the same every day or is it fluid and ever-changing? Take thirty minutes to an hour, clear your schedule, and sit with a journal. Write about your dream work day, the work culture that lights you up the most, and the different ways you want your business to support your daily routine and not the other way around. Get really clear and push the boundaries. What does fulfillment in your daily work life look like to you?

Let's put it to paper, shall we? Time to architect your aligned work environment.

Your Dream Work Culture:

Let's start with what you don't want based off of experiences in a past job.

What is the one policy from a past job you did not agree with?

What was your biggest work culture pain point on a day to day basis?

What didn't sit right with you when it came to boss-employee relationships?

Where was an area that you felt as if you had no freedom?

```

```

With the out-of-alignment factors of a past work environment listed above, let's start to create new policies and culture. Answer these questions with what feels good in your gut. Follow your intuition here and do not question it or feel foolish for thinking something like this is possible. Write down all of your dreams without judgment!

What are your ideal daily work hours?

```

```

Would you like to work out of an office everyday or have your team remote?

```

```

How many days a week do you want to work?

```

```

When you envision yourself showing up to a meeting, what are you wearing?

What tone of communication via email makes you feel inspired and connected in business?

How do you want your employees to talk about their job behind your back?

These answers will illuminate what your dream work environment is and, since you are an entrepreneur, you get to implement that dream.

When I started Scout's Agency, I wanted my emails to have a very personal touch to them. I email my clients with enthusiasm, exclamation marks, and depending on the client, I will start an email with Hi, beauty! It took my first employee a bit of time to realize she didn't have to infuse dryness and rigidity into her emails. We utilize smiley faces constantly, are warm, and talk like we normally would over dinner just with a hint of professionalism to communicate we are the experts and the guides in our field. That is a decision I made because I wanted to show up as myself in my daily correspondence, not as some cut and dry robot. And as the owner of the business, I got to implement that. In return, my clients feel as if we care about them and my employees feel like they can be themselves.

Other ways Scout's Agency follows my dream work environment:

1. On Fridays, we end work at 3:00 pm.

2. We have no official vacation policy nor a certain amount of lead time you have to request off. If their friends are doing an impromptu weekend in Palm Springs and there is nothing pressing happening on Friday—great! I tell them I am jealous, to have fun, and I'll chat with them on Monday.

3. Work hours are 9:00 am-5:00 pm, but lunch time is flexible and my employees regularly tell me, I have therapy scheduled at 2:00 today, or my cousin is in town so I am going to take a longer lunch today.

4. We all work remotely! I used to have an office but after the pandemic hit, I realized my love for working from home. For the foreseeable future, our work will be remote.

5. Dress code if no clients are present is usually matching sweatsuits.

6. Mental health is openly talked about in team meetings as we are all here to support one another's emotional wellbeing.

7. If they didn't sleep well the night before, they take a nap during the day. The amount of times I get a Slack saying, Super tired and hitting a wall, going to take a nap. I'll let you know when I am back online. It happens a lot because my employees are comfortable knowing that I want them to take

1. care of themselves. When I am hitting a wall, the last thing I want to do is to continue working. I want to take a nap. So, my team knows they can do the same so that they can recharge and be up and running in a better mental state.

2. It's just a lot of freedom as you are deducing here! The self-employed mindset is what I want my team members to have. It's not for all, but those that it does work for soar.

You are building and creating as an entrepreneur, so make sure when you start developing your work culture and your daily flow that you infuse it with your dream scenario. You can cut the excess fat of how things were once done, ditch the shoulds, and live in the abundance of what your reality in your business gets to be, not what it should be.

The Lesson: You get to create the work culture you want to work in, whether that means half-days on Fridays or empowering your team to take initiative. You get to structure your life, not some corporate handbook.

AN EMOTIONAL LAW OF ENTREPRENEURSHIP: YOU AREN'T HERE TO FOLLOW RULES. YOU ARE HERE TO MAKE YOUR OWN.

Lesson #15:

You Aren't Here to Follow Rules

"Having studied broadcasting journalism to be a sports newscaster, I somehow ended up knee deep in the fashion retail world with hopes to open a brick and mortar store. At the age of 24, despite everyone's opinions about the death of retail, I took the risk and followed my heart. 8 years later, I still own and operate my store that has not only survived a pandemic, but cultivated a community that has allowed me to have the confidence to launch a clothing brand that I also cherish madly. What initially was a detour, has turned into a light that ignites a fire in my soul daily and I couldn't ask for anything more."

-Lily Adel, Founder CLYQUE the Label + ELLE A. Boutique

Let's talk about the phrase *have to*. It creeps into our daily vernacular and repeats itself consistently and holds more emotional weight than any other exclamation that decorates our daily lives. If you aren't speaking your list of have tos or shoulds out loud, they are definitely taking up large amounts of real estate in your mind. And the scary part about the times we do invite have to into our plans, we often don't even realize we are doing it.

> *I am sure the following sounds quite familiar:*
> *I have to call her back.*
> *I have to go to her birthday dinner.*
> *I have to pick up dinner for her because she is having a rough day.*
> *I have to send out those emails tonight.*
> *I have to drive up to Los Angeles for that meeting.*
> *I have to be more emotionally available for my partner.*
> *I have to get in a full day's work today.*
> *I have to go for a walk in the mornings.*
> *I have to drink more water.*
> *I have to meditate.*
> *I have to cut dairy out of my diet.*
> *I have to graduate college.*
> *I have to get a job as a lawyer.*
> *I have to follow the path my parents want me to follow.*

You know these statements because they are the decision makers in the actions you take proceeding the thought of what you think you should do. And when you add up all of the things you have done because you felt as if you have to do them, how big does that mountain look?

I was feeling extremely out of alignment one week: anxious, stressed, and tired. I knew I had more social obligations than normal with my in-laws being in town, so I just marked it off as

137

having more on my schedule that week. My mindset coach heard something different. In our voice notes back and forth, she pointed out that I kept talking about the things that I was doing that week as events on my calendar that I have to do. After realizing that the majority of my energy that week was spent on things that I felt I had some emotional obligation toward out of duty, I was able to reassess: Do I want to do these things? And if I do, then it's *not I have to do this but rather I get to do this.*

Let's get micro real quick though. Think about the snapshot of your calendar. Bring up the image of your beautifully color coded calendar. Is it balanced? Are there too many social obligations and not enough unwinding time? Do you have too many sales calls on Tuesday and not enough time to work out? Is Friday night family dinner pulling at your obligation strings versus your excitement? Is your social life overtaking your weeks? Is your nine-to-five filled with obligations and duties towards someone else's higher plan? Does the course you're taking, fractioned up into little chunks of time on a calendar, follow your own set of rules on how you want to live your life or someone else's?

Then ask yourself: Do I want to do these things? In your heart, when you think about the tasks, responsibilities, social commitments, and overall flow of your schedule, does it excite you or fill you with dread?

There is this invisible rule that we as a society have self-imposed quite falsely on one another. This invisible false rule is that we have to do the things we don't want to do. That life is a series of unavoidable, joyless tasks. That having responsibility and being an adult is working to make ends meet, in a repetitive fashion until you retire.

I am here to set you free, emotional entrepreneur. Entrepreneurship takes this self-imposed and life-destructive viewpoint and smashes it into a little million pieces. In those pieces, you are able to rebuild your life not out of *have tos* but out of things you get to do.

An emotional law of entrepreneurship: You aren't here to follow rules. You are here to make your own.

This gets to look in so many nuanced and grand ways. You want to start work at 10:30 am? Go for it. You want to demolish the business casual dress code at your office? Go for it. You want to drop out of college to pursue your start-up? Go for it (with the right amount of calculated risk—see Lesson #8). You want to limit the amount of times you spend on social activities? Go for it. You want to sell your pottery instead of go to law school? Go for it. You want to tell your family you won't be able to attend weekly dinner for the next month? Go for it. You want to have the audacity to show up every single day stoked about what you do because you built it? Fucking go for it. I am rooting for you.

Entrepreneurship is emotional because there is no real rule book. The entire spirit of being an entrepreneur is that you create your own. That through trial and error, you will stumble upon what the right balance of what makes your business work and what fuels your passion on a daily basis. That if you are willing to fail and pivot and swim with the waves, your own rule book will appear. Following the rules of someone else is working within someone else's framework of what works for them or for the masses on some organizational scale. Following your rules allows you to breath magic into the creation of your life and your business. It allows you to be the creator of your Google calendar. And we all know, your Google calendar is a representation of the quality of your daily life.

Now, as much as I am urging you to create and follow your own rules, because that is what will define you as an entrepreneur, I also live within the same reality you do and there are things that are unavoidable that we must complete even if we don't want to.

For example: taxes, firing an employee, picking up the workload when an employee randomly quits, or taking a meeting here and there that doesn't serve you in the moment.

Creating your own rule book doesn't mean that your life will be depleted of *shoulds* or *have tos*. It just means that the shoulds of your life are significantly diminished and the majority of where your energy goes and flows is not in the dreaded obligations but rather in the areas you are excited to contribute to.

And when work gets overwhelming and your mind gets over-taken by stress, it is easy for you to identify your workload as a should, as an invisible rule that you must get done. It is here that we get to work with mindset and shift our emotional perception of that daunting to do list. Because in our lives, you don't have to do anything. You do get to do it.

As I created my own rule book for my life, disregarding all of the other rules I was given as a child, such as graduate college, work-ing a corporate job, not putting your mental illness on the inter-net, I realized that responsibility still lives in my corner. Responsi-bility will always live in your corner. It is the thing that asks you to rise to the occasion to live out your full and vast potential. The rule book we are given paints responsibility within the lands of shoulds. We get to reclaim our relationship to the responsibilities in our business. We get to wake up and say, *"I get to do this today."*

> *Have 50 emails you have to answer? I get to answer all of my emails today!*
> *Have to go to the bank? I get to go to the bank because I am the owner of a business account!*
> *Have to take 5 sales calls today? I get to talk to people who are interested in my services!*
> *Have to have a tough talk with your team? I get to help guide my team towards success!*
> *Have to get a presentation out to a client tonight? I get to*

create something for my client that will serve their brand!
Have to file your taxes? I get to file taxes that are more
complex because I own my own business!

When we create our own rule book, we shed the rules that don't serve us, we create new ones that do, and we reframe our perspective around the inevitable tasks that at times can feel daunting, overwhelming, or tedious.

The result? Our energetic balance is peaking toward the side of fulfillment and excitement. The roadmap is expansive because we know it is unlimited. We follow our own rules that in return make up the cal invites of our lives.

Let's all get to the end of our lives and be able to confidently speak Frank Sinatra's words: I did it my way.

The Lesson: The moment you let go of the rules you should be following or feel as if you have to follow is the moment you create your unique magic.

WHEN YOU ALLOW
YOURSELF SPACE
TO BE, YOU SHOW
UP EMOTIONALLY
PREPARED FOR LIFE'S
FUTURE COURSE.

Lesson #16:

Cultivate Morning and Night Routines

"The structures you create around your morning and evening rituals can transform the way you move through the world. Small, consistent daily actions add up overtime. Taking time for non-reactive rituals and committing to honor the space you create to put yourself first allows you to show up for your work and other people around you."

-Dianna Cohen, Founder and CEO of Crown Affair

There is so much beauty in the awakening and in the winding down. Our days are framed with transitions, that if respected, can turn into the most sacred and fruitful times. Moments where we listen to birds sing their first note and times where we feel the absence of sun to settle us down. Silence infuses itself into our minds. Our essence is moving between states. One building on the other.

I am talking about the thoroughly sought after morning and night routine, the art that I believe I have mastered despite its ever evolution.

If skincare routines were for the influencer, morning and night routines (specifically morning) are for the entrepreneur. We have listened to countless podcasts where the host is extracting their guest's morning routine down to the minute details. We have also heard that one of the common weaves amongst all highly successful people is that they have a decently strict morning routine.

I fell in love with morning routines in middle school. I remember timing out my morning to the minute; four minutes to shower, two to get dressed, three to do my hair, and so forth. I was always diligent with my morning space when it came to being quick with my time, but that diligence turned into a sort of spiritual expression over the years. As my responsibility changed from sixth grade homework to running my own business, that hour to two hours in the mornings became the framework of which I was to set up my mindset for the working day, the coming home to myself moment, the time I got to connect within sans distractions.

There are a few main benefits to cultivating a morning and night routine for your sanity as well as for your soul. As an entrepreneur, you are never really off the clock. There is no nine to five requirement of you, no machine you can go to to clock out, exit the building, and free the confines of your mind from anything work related. Your work becomes a continuing through line of your life and while I always advocate for turning work off at a certain point

144

of the day, in the beginning, when passion is high and excitement is rampant, it can be tough. A "touching base" with yourself first thing in the morning and last thing at night can provide that space for you to tune back into you. Not your sales of the day, not your calls that you will have, not your inbox, which is never ending. These are the moments just for you.

When you carve out space for your night routine, you allow yourself to enter your slumbering dreams without the last thought in your head being an angry email you just had to read before shutting your eyes. You can enter your subconscious from a state of relaxation and gratitude versus over stimulation. This will also help you sleep better. By turning off work at night, settling into a routine, shedding layers of stress, and incorporating moments of stillness, you will not only doze off more quickly but you will settle that constant loop of your to-dos for the next day allowing those to be on a break from the forefront of your attention.

And with a better, rested night sleep, comes a better awakened morning. Moving through a morning routine allows you to do one main thing: connect with just yourself so that you feel grounded, inspired, and ready. The mindset it cultivates within will allow you that strengthening shield when you do go to open your inbox and are exposed to everyone else's energy, asks, and demands. You open your inbox rooted in your root and solar plexus chakra versus being unprepared, half awake, and alerted to something via email you weren't exactly in the mind frame to handle.

This played out so clearly for me recently. As you'll read later on in this chapter as I outline my morning routine, I do not look at my phone for the first hour to two hours of the day. I set aside that time just for me—for journaling, for going on my morning walk, for picking cards, for showering, for moving through my skincare routine. I also usually wake up before my alarm clock, which allows me a moment to consciously not look at my notifications as I go to turn the future alarm off.

One morning, I slept well into my alarm clock. As I went to turn it off, half asleep and groggy, I saw a notification about an email from my graphic designer who was in the process of rebranding Scout's Agency's website. She had emailed me the mood board and logo options to kickstart the rebrand and I was excited. I told myself that even though my energy wanted me to check out the different logos, color palettes, and design inspiration now, I would wait until after I had at least journaled and picked cards. And since my excitement couldn't be contained, I journaled quickly and picked cards hastily with divided attention. When I was barely a few sips into my coffee, twenty five minutes after I had woken up, I opened my phone and checked my email. As I went to open my graphic designer's email, I saw another one that I thought looked odd. Curiosity and anxiety pulled me to open that email, in which a weird miscommunication between my team and a podcast host revealed itself.

That was all it took. I was anxious and I entered the rabbit hole. I responded hastily to correct the miscommunication, I moved on to check the rest of my inbox (which did include the rebrand mood-board), then I moved to the Okay Sis email account to find out I had missed an invoice, then I moved to Instagram, and then I moved to text messages where my sister had asked me to get her something that day for the podcast. I hadn't even been awake for thirty minutes and suddenly every notification, to-do list, demand, another woman's photo in a bikini on a beach, and 360 snapshot of my business were bombarding my mind. I wasn't prepared. I hadn't centered myself. I hadn't connected to myself and my soul. I hadn't woken up and been grateful for the fact that I had awoken to another day. I woke up and went into reactive mode by giving myself to everyone else in my sphere.

I recognized after ten minutes of jumping from app to app in my phone the levels of anxiety and chaos I was feeling inside. I wasn't leveled or confident. I had opened Pandora's Box and didn't know how to close it so that I could shower in peace, make breakfast, feel connected, and give my puppy snuggles before I started my day.

As I prayed to God to recenter my morning and reset my emotional foundation so that I didn't bring this energy into the rest of my day, I realized that this was the ultimate lesson. I always preached a morning routine where I didn't look at my phone for the first hour or two of the day because it made me feel good in the moment, but the second I realized how destabilizing it was if I didn't partake in that morning routine was the moment I solidified the importance of connecting inwards first thing in the morning versus offering yourself to the external world.

Now I don't just preach it. It's my new non-negotiable.

So how does one set up systems of routines for sacred still time with oneself? Morning and night routines are completely individualized and there is no one-size-fits all but as just illustrated there is one huge, important, main rule to morning and night routines: you cannot look at your phone. Everything else is flexible, but this, my dear ones, I can now say confidently is the foundation for all successful morning and night routines.

Let's walk through my current routines, knowing that they are evolving and constantly in flux with things being added in or subtracted.

6:00-6:30 am: I wake up naturally, which prompts my puppy Luna to continue to awaken me by giving me kisses all over my face.

I make myself a warm cup of water with lemon to rev my metabolism, detox my liver, support my digestion, and rehydrate my body.

I open up the back door for Luna to go out to the bathroom and step outside to breathe in some fresh air for a few moments.

147

Once I have finished my warm cup of water with lemon, I pour myself my first cup of coffee.

6:15-6:45 am: I write my morning pages. Every morning, I write for one to two pages in my journal with no specific theme or journal prompt. I free flow with my subconscious. Sometimes, nothing profound comes out, and I am just writing about how I slept the night before, what I am excited about for the day, etc. Other times, massive life choices come through me. Like with this book, I planned the entire marketing plan half awake just writing in my journal. It spilled out of me even though that was not my intention for that morning's session. Morning pages are a beautiful brain dump to either let go of energy to start the day or ignite energy to start the day through processing, tapping into the subconscious, and connecting within.

7:20 am: Go for a power walk. I put on a podcast (the only time I pick up my phone but I do not check my text messages, social media, or inbox...I just go immediately to the podcast app!)—usually a business podcast or an interview where I admire the guest's career to get me in the entrepreneurial spirit—and just walk and walk and walk.

8:00 am: Shower, put a body oil on, get dressed, morning skincare routine, etc.

8:30 am: Make breakfast and pour my second cup of coffee, which consists of either eggs, sautéed greens, and chickpeas or oatmeal with berries or chia seed pudding with bananas. While I eat breakfast, I am either listening to another podcast or reading an intriguing article by an outlet like Vogue.

8:45 am: Check my phone! First I start with text messages, then move to Instagram and then to podcast download stats.

9:00 am: Open up my computer, check my email, and start my day of work.

This is the basic framework for my days. I add in things at times too—like pulling cards from my Inner Compass Deck before starting morning pages, or if my body is not in the mood for a walk, I will read a book or do a deep meditation. But do notice: I grab my phone to put a podcast on at 7:20 am but do not check my phone until 8:30-8:45 am every day. Two hours of complete disconnected bliss.

My night routine, which is less extensive but designed for optimal relaxation:

8:00 pm: Make my sleepy time tea with honey. As I let it sit and cool down, I will go do my skincare routine and wash my feet.

8:10 pm - 9:00 pm: Drink my tea with my husband on the couch watching a TV show.

8:30 pm: Set alarm and put my phone away.

9:00 pm - 10:00 pm: Read my book in bed sans phone.

This may seem overwhelming, too disciplined, and one too many steps (and believe me, I left out a lot, such as when I take my vitamins in the morning and the extensive order of my skincare routine, etc!). Don't be discouraged by the fleshed out version of my routines. These took years to cultivate and get just right. If you can commit to the first twenty minutes of your day without your phone reading, meditating, walking outside on the grass, or journaling, then bravo! The energy you will cultivate within that twenty minutes will lead you through your day with a sturdy foundation. After making those first twenty minutes an automatic habit where your mind and body begins to crave it, add things on—a walk, a podcast listen, or space to really make yourself breakfast and eat in peace and intention.

We often get lost in the stimuli of our modern working worlds. And while I love when I am in my masculine and productivity is flowing through my veins (I wouldn't be an entrepreneur if that didn't light me up), I also love tapping into my inner world without all the external noise. This internal tap brings you to your passion and your business with clarity and a readiness. When you allow yourself space to be, you show up emotionally prepared to life's future course.

The Lesson: Take care of yourself. You can expand your dreams into reality with more sparkle if you set up systems to keep your engine going.

BEING AN ENTREPRENEUR ISN'T BRANDING OR EVEN COMING UP WITH A MILLION-DOLLAR IDEA. BEING AN ENTREPRENEUR IS WALKING THROUGH THE FIRE WITH YOUR HEAD HELD HIGH.

Lesson #17:

Pivot, Don't Give Up

"One of the hardest and most rewarding things I've done in my life thus far is to let go of what I thought my life would be and make room for possibilities beyond what my mind could imagine. Our minds are so limited - often times they're just running on programming and limiting beliefs. So when anything in life comes up or in 'unexpectedly,' I get excited to try it on and feel whether this 'new thing' is a deeper expression of my soul. Almost 30, the podcast I host with Krista Williams, is the perfect example of what happens when I say yes to something I could have never dreamed up in my own mind."

-Lindsey Simcik, co-host of Almost 30 Podcast

I sat in a Zoom with my sister on a Sunday afternoon staring at a very low number of women who had signed up for our virtual event. It was a week before the event and we started to panic. What if no one showed up? We had major headlining guests like Natalie Mariduena and Brittany Xavier that we didn't want to let down. We had invested $1000 into custom graphics for the event that we didn't want to go to waste. We had been selling tickets on our Instagram and podcast for the last three weeks and the result of our intention to bring the community together resulted in confusion toward low ticket sales.

In that moment, I realized we were facing the pressure point of what it means to be an entrepreneur: how we handled that last week leading up to the event would say everything about us as brand builders, business owners, and community leaders.

This is a truth I hold near and dear to my heart: building a brand makes you a brand builder, curating an Instagram feed makes you a creative, and gaining a new client makes you a sales manager, but handling the fires makes you an entrepreneur.

Up until your first *"this isn't working"* or *"wow, that was a big fuck up"* or *"this client is really angry at me"* or *"we didn't hit our revenue projections,"* it's all creative, inspiring fun. It's creating your logo, your brand colors for your website, your Instagram feed. It's designing your first product and getting samples in the mail to test out. It's writing all the blog posts. It's dreaming of future successes. It's seeing the first small steps live outside of your mind.

And then, the reality of business settles in: things don't always unfold as planned. You might lose three main clients in one week, dropping your monthly revenue significantly. Your manufacturers might ship you the wrong product and now you're sitting on three hundred sweatshirts in the wrong color. Your launch doesn't sell out. Your event isn't selling tickets. Your employee quits suddenly. In these moments you have two choices: gear up and walk through the fire or quit.

It's the ones that exhibit the former action that are still around today—the ones you have heard of or the ones that populate your social media feed or the ones in your friend circle. They all chose, time and time and time again, to suit up, take a deep breath, know shit's about to get uncomfortable, and step up to the plate.

Because on the other end of that fire? First, entrepreneurs always know that survival before, during, and after walking through the fire is a guarantee—even if worst case scenario the business fails due to that fire. You will survive the hard shit of your life and on the other end is clarity, strength, and a beautiful vision for the future.

Our live event taught us so many things for Okay Sis Podcast. First, we rolled up our sleeves and asked what we could do to sell those tickets. What was available to us at our fingertips? What were ways to market the event that felt good to us? What were creative ways we could hype up our community?

We did giveaways, posted Instagram stories about the event, and DMed our sisterhood. We also decided that we didn't want to go into our event stressed about the numbers of tickets we sold or who would or would not be there. We wanted to just spend a few hours with the sisters who listen to our podcast and were a part of our community. We wanted to hang with them.

We talked to other people in the industry who were really impressed by the amount of tickets we had been able to sell. Selling virtual events in early 2021 was a mission and a half. People had Zoom fatigue, virtual events were taking over people's weekends, and no one really wanted to *pay*.

So, we shifted our expectation of the market. Our ticket sales that we initially felt were low for a four-hour virtual event that wasn't an educational workshop was pretty damn good for the industry. We started to be proud.

And then, up until the last minute, we sold more tickets, making our bottom line amazing. That initial number we dismally looked at a week prior was now exciting us. We had an incredible virtual event, got to talk to so many women in our community, had rad chats with Natalie Mariduena and Brittany Xavier, gave three robust giveaways to our community, laughed, drank champagne, got into a mental health workshop with Madhappy, and had a good fucking time.

But the point here is that on that Sunday, fear crept in and we asked ourselves, "Is our community not as strong as we think it is? Is this event going to be a total and utter failure? Are we going to embarrass ourselves? Are people going to think we are frauds?" It was in the moment after we asked those questions where we invited fear and self-doubt to live heavy on our hearts that we shifted and buckled up.

Those are the sacred moments of entrepreneurship. It is the way you handle those moments that define you as an entrepreneur and will eventually define the health and success of your business. Being an entrepreneur isn't branding or even coming up with a million dollar idea. Being an entrepreneur is walking through the fire and walking through it with your head held high.

When things don't go as planned or when expectations are not met, know in your bones that giving up is not an option. Once you make that commitment to yourself, assess how you can pivot. For me and Mady, we realized that virtual events were not going to be one of our main revenue streams. We loved being in the energy of our sisterhood because as a podcast all we truly see are the number of downloads on a screen. Seeing the women who listen to us each week was more rewarding than ever. After the event, we decided to pivot away from virtual events and throw more spontaneous free happy hours for our community to join in so we get face time with our community. We also started questioning things like, What does our community want to purchase from us? What is the sweet spot of price within our community? Do they want sweatshirts? Do they want coaching programs? Do they want workshops? How can we best support our community at the exact price point that feels good to them?

Asking these questions is what will allow me and Mady to put our energy toward things that really impact our community and light us up. We pivoted but we didn't give up.

This example is on a smaller scale, but within every launch, product, service, or revenue stream you offer, when things aren't going as planned, catastrophe starts overtaking your ego. We get into the weeds with our businesses and sometimes don't take the zoomed out perspective, the big picture that knows that things are going to be okay, that things aren't as big or scary as our anxiety is telling us, and that no one is watching us as closely as we are watching ourselves.

Every time you don't give up and then make a conscious effort to pivot with your future goals is the moment you get closer to the gold. Pivoting allows you to refine, refine, refine. It cuts out everything that isn't working in your business and frees up time, space, and energy for the things that will move your revenue and your dreams along.

Let's take Scout's Agency as an example. Here are a few of my major pivots that landed me to where I am today:

- *Opening up my roster to women who weren't podcasters:* In the beginning of Scout's Agency, I represented only female podcasters. In a concentrated effort to niche down, which totally worked for me in the long-run, I started hitting walls when it came to my pricing. The podcasters I were serving

156

were those that weren't with a network and so the majority of them were not in a position where the podcast was bringing in enough revenue to hire outside help in a larger capacity, such as myself. My monthly revenue prices were under $1000/month—even the traditional PR package. I quickly saw that even though I had set out to niche down when it came to the type of clients I represented, that that niche was going to hold back my revenue goals. I pivoted and became a female-focused PR agency that specializes in securing women as a guest on podcasts to tell their stories. I got to represent ridiculously rad women and was able to up my monthly retainers significantly.

- *Establishing time commitment contracts:* In the beginning of running Scout's Agency, I was on month-to-month retainers with my clients. That means that at any given moment they could drop off. And that means my future revenue was difficult to predict, causing difficulty for me to establish future planning and goals. One month, I lost a few major clients after having just hired my first employee. That month-to-month contract was a way to bring clients in, easing their fear of being tied down to a monthly retainer. I quickly saw that while that might be serving their fears in the short run, it wasn't allowing me to dig deep into my work the way I knew I could to bring them the best opportunities. It also wasn't setting myself up as a serious agency. I immediately implemented three to six month contracts and will no longer do a shorter contract deal.

- *Working remotely after having an office for a year:* The pandemic was the biggest pivot moment in our personal lives as well as in our business lives. Up until quarantine hit in March 2020, Scout's Agency was run in-person in an office. We quickly pivoted to being remote and figuring out what that meant: was having daily check-in meetings best? Weekly meetings? How organized should our Slack channels be? After pivoting and figuring out what works best for my team, I decided to not renew my lease on the office. As we saw the success of all working from home, I pivoted to remote work only. This allowed me to bring in team members that weren't local to San Diego, something we wouldn't have been able to do if we were still in-person.

Sometimes the pivot is small—charging $9.99 for your product instead of $12.99—and sometimes the pivot is big, where you have to rethink your entire revenue model from wholesale to direct-to-consumer. Whatever the pivot is, know that it is always available to you. Have the foresight to see when emotions are high and fear is pumping through your veins that there are ways to adapt and be fluid. There are always ways to refine and change course.

And as the entrepreneur, you walk through the fire knowing that as you emerge from the smoke, there will be new writing on the wall. And with that, you will get back to work.

The Lesson: Don't be so attached to the initial plan; let the universe show you where you should go.

WHAT IF YOU ENJOYED THE BUILD AND NOT THE LARGER-THAN-LIFE REPUTATION?

Lesson #18:

Celebrate The Small Wins

"We've got to celebrate our magic, in the middle of life's messes. All we know we've got for sure is today... and isn't that simple, precious gift worthy of celebration? A good hair day. Actually finishing a book you started. Finally saying 'no' to that brunch with those terrible people you always wished you would say 'no' to. These little wins make up the sum of your life. Please don't get so caught up trying to reach that big, sexy, ever-unattainable peak of your life's ideal mountaintop... that you forget to look back often, and enjoy the view. You did that, step-by-step! You, my friend, deserve wine. Or chocolate. Or both."

- Zuri Hall, Emmy Award-Winning TV Host, "Access Hollywood" & NBC's "American Ninja Warrior"

We have talked a lot about when things don't go exactly as planned in entrepreneurship and how to tackle that emotionally with strong armor. And maybe you are weighed down and are looking for the beauty in all of this. I am here to tell you that there is another aspect to the dream building process that is so much larger, expansive, and exciting than the fires or the tedious start-up tasks. There is another aspect that creates 90% of your business yet I would confidently bet that you aren't shedding light on these daily occurrences. They most likely live in the shadows, repressed as minor details, or shoved to the side as "no big deal." If you become a master at realizing and promoting these aspects of your business, you will enjoy the daily nuanced steps so thoroughly that they will fill your core up with fulfillment and acceptance for the stage you are currently in, while also holding space for future dreams. You will awaken to each day with an excitement to get to work because you will learn to enjoy the process so much more than you yearn for that perceived final destination.

How?

You must celebrate the small wins.

I am notorious for celebrating the small wins - each and every single spec of good news is internalized, celebrated, and shared. When I say small, I mean if Okay Sis Podcast gets ten more downloads on an episode which in turn breaks our download record - regardless of the fact that the record was only broken by ten downloads - I am celebrating by texting my sister with ten million exclamation marks and uppercase letters. If I am on a sales call with a potential client for Scout's Agency and they say they don't have the financial means to commit to a three or six month contract but express that the moment they do they want to go with my agency over another - I am celebrating. If a podcaster I admire wants to have me on as a guest - I am celebrating. If I finally cleared my inbox after days of it piling up - I am celebrating. If I get a DM from someone who listens to SCOUT Podcast, my solo podcast where I ramble about mental health, saying that my latest episode filled her up with so much hope and strength for the future - I am celebrating. If I get my client as a guest on her dream podcast - I am celebrating. If I worked out three days in a row, I am celebrating. If someone I admire took the time to email me back, even if the email is to let me know they are passing on the opportunity, I am celebrating.

There is always time for the big celebrations; the signing of your biggest client, the booking of your ultimate podcast guest, the moment you increase your salary significantly, the email that says you were nominated for Forbes 30 Under 30. All of that is delicious and great and expansive and major. But the small wins? They will keep the wheels of your mind turning with an excitement and a fulfillment that is long lasting and will embellish the quality of your life. The small wins are the way you enjoy the here and now without living in the longing for your future goals to arrive.

When you start your business, especially when you start your business, everything is enticing and exciting. Your first Etsy order! Your first website page view! Your first inquiry from a potential client! Your first retailer interested in your product! Your first mockup of your book cover! It is all so flabbergastingly exciting that you can't help but be completely lit up amongst all of your firsts.

In the beginning of starting Scout's Agency, we poured ourselves a glass of wine every time we signed a client. We jumped up and down and screamed when Catt Sadler said she wanted us to run her podcast drive. We bombarded our #wins Slack channel with exclamation marks and GIFs of champagne popping. We were utterly stoked about everything.

And then the wins became our norm.

As the months went on and signing clients became a much more normal occurrence (good problem to have - I know!), the celebrations started weaning away. I would sign a client, notify my team, and move on with my day. I was past the honeymoon phase, and just like being in a long term relationship, you have to keep the sparks flying. I had to recenter myself and feel the gratitude for all of the things happening in my business - I had to get back to celebrating.

In today's modern society, we have a tendency to live in the future when it comes to our career. Our success is determined on our future promotion, the day we sell our business, the month our revenue hits X amount of dollars, the moment a celebrity wants to endorse our product, the day we hit 10k followers on Instagram, or the moment we become a New York Times bestselling author. We look to these external metrics of success to finally fill us with a sense of happiness, security, and fulfillment despite the fact that we know, deep down, that these external metrics are moving targets, that they are ever changing, and the minute we hit one and share it to our social media we are already on our way to create another one in our minds, completely dismissing the moment of happiness, security, and fulfillment we were expecting it to flood us with when we initially set the goal. It is a chase that is endlessly never filling up our cup.

But what if the minute-to-minute mundane wins were the ones you lived for? What if your day wasn't waiting for the big yearly revenue goal or the call from Sephora that they want to carry your product? What if you saw the small moments that make up and build your dreams as the most precious ones of all? What if you enjoyed the build and not the larger than life reputation?

When it comes to celebrating the small wins, it can feel out of your comfort zone if you're used to large and intense metrics of success. The key to celebrating a small win is practicing a shift in perspective, applying non-judgment, and sharing with a loved one.

A shift in perspective: If you have been conditioned to view the wins in your life as the larger milestones that were given to you by external validation - the college admission, the graduation diploma, the job offer, the promotion - then the smaller ones that you usually skip over will be easy to miss. To start feeling internally proud of yourself for the nuanced details of your day, we have to first acknowledge them. Start by listing out five things that you did today that you are proud of.

If you need help coming up with the small wins, here are a few examples to get you started:

> I sat down to eat a full breakfast without distractions before I started work!
> I sent out my first sales proposal to a prospective client!
> I got a DM that someone likes my branding!
> I got through all of my emails today!
> I started a TikTok account for my business!
> I secured a potential sales call with a dream client!
> I have a customer that is interested in my product!

When you start shifting your perspective that the metric of success is really the combination of small wins you experience on a day to day basis, start micro - really micro.

Five small wins that I am celebrating from today's work day:

1. _____
2. _____
3. _____
4. _____
5. _____

View your small wins without judgment: As you wrote that list, did that self-doubting voice come up in your head? The one that says, "These are no big deal. You don't deserve to celebrate these.

You didn't sell your company. You aren't featured in Forbes. You don't run a six-figure business. Keep your head down. Get back to work. You can celebrate when Google comes and wants to buy your app."

That is the voice that will rob you of enjoying the process which is synonymous with your life. It will keep you from walking into a room and owning your progress while also finding immense fulfillment in the day-to-day. If your inner critic becomes heightened when celebrating the small wins, you get to look at your list through a lens of non-judgment.

One person's small win might be that they got out of bed and made themselves a matcha latte. Another person's small win might be that they signed a new client.

Where your small win lies on the spectrum doesn't matter. What matters is how you feel about it. So once you start recognizing the wins as they come about throughout the day, practice non-judgment if your inner critic thinks you're being too congratulatory.

You are out there doing it. Every single day. And that deserves to be celebrated. You deserve to be celebrated.

Share with a loved one or a team member: Sharing wins with those you love or those you work with is the best way to keep the momentum going! Spreading the excitement and the pride with others will help you internalize your achievements since you are sharing them out loud. Now, sharing your five small wins every single day with a loved one might be overkill. Definitely give yourself a high five when they happen and when one win comes along that you are super stoked on, share it! Text it to a friend! Let your partner know at the end of the day!

The other night, I was really proud of one page in this book. I told my husband with a smile so wide. He said, *"I love watching you be proud of the things that you do."* When you celebrate your achievements, it gives others permission to celebrate theirs.

The ripple effect? We all get to view the mundane details that would usually go overlooked as exciting, celebratory, and fulfilling. The journey becomes the goal not the destination - that's just the cherry on top. You don't want to be Emily Weiss. You want to build Glossier.

Remind yourself: You do the things you do because you love to do them in the moment not because of the external validation they will one day give you. The external validation is the bonus, not your salary.

And the way we stay engaged throughout the process and provide ourselves with fulfillment right here and now, regardless of whether you just started your business Instagram account or if you just hit five figure months, is to celebrate the small wins along the way.

The smaller the better, the more delicious, the sweeter the path.

The Lesson: Open your eyes to the little daily joys so that the journey is fulfilling.

NOTHING CAN
TAKE AWAY YOUR
FREEDOM. YOU
CHOSE TO BE HERE,
AND THERE IS
BEAUTIFUL POWER
IN THAT CHOICE.

Lesson #19:

Responsibility Is Scary, And You Were Born For It

"Spending time thinking that you're running out of time is distracting you from living out your greatness."

-Olamide Olowe, Founder & CEO of TOPICALS

Scenario #1: I remember the moment a client of mine said they wanted to sign a contract to work together for the rest of 2020. It was around April when they delivered the good news which would make this contract my longest one I had ever drafted, signed, and committed to within my agency. It was a huge win and as I signed the contract, I was riddled with fear.

Scenario #2: I was falling behind on my daily tasks for client work as my responsibilities as a CEO got greater within the agency. Sales calls, networking calls, podcast interviews, invoicing, running payroll, and updating our website were starting to overflow my Google calendar. I decided it was time to hire a second employee to help keep up with the weekly client pitching. My stomach dropped, my face was flushed, and my heart wouldn't stop racing when I sent a job offer out.

Scenario #3: I lost four clients unexpectedly and watched my monthly revenue dwindle down to a number I was uncomfortable with. I looked at the salary requirements of my employees and calculated the loss we were going to take that month. My roster of clients made my eyes bleed as I scrutinized how short the list was. It was up to me to replenish it - and I was on a tight timeline.

Responsibility is scary. It doesn't matter if the deal is technically a win - you got an investor, you signed your biggest client, your product is now in Urban Outfitters - sometimes the win can feel big and heavy and can knock you out of your comfort zone. Because when you score a big deal in your business, now it's time to show up and not just show up tomorrow, but show up for the foreseeable future. It is the biggest reality of entrepreneurship: you are responsible for this ship.

Out of that responsibility comes beautiful truths: you are never truly chained down to any deal or path your business takes. You can always change course to reflect what is in your highest alignment. Nothing can take away your freedom. You chose to be here and there is beautiful power in that choice.

But, at the end of the day, your emotional success as an entrepreneur will depend on how you handle this responsibility and how you, hopefully, rise to the occasion instead of back away from intensity. First, you have to feel the fear, anxiety, and total panic that comes with stepping out of your comfort zone and into your next up level.

I felt bad when I felt the all encompassing fear that visited when I signed the contract to represent my client for the rest of the year. It seemed like a big deal, because it was, but it was also in the midst of the pandemic where jobs were scarce and businesses were closing. I was sitting here scared of opportunity. I was sitting here scared of predictable revenue. I was sitting here scared of the responsibility I was taking on when so many others were praying to be in my position.

And that my dear is one-hundred percent okay. Fear will visit when you are entering into the next level of your business and anxiety will warn you that you are entering into the unknown. To shame ourselves for feeling the total and utter responsibility of responsibility before accepting its invitation with open arms is counterintuitive to your emotional process.

Feel the fear, feel the anxiety, feel the uncertainty. And then, sign the contract and show up to the version of yourself you know the world is ready for.

And as you show up and master the next level, which will then become your new comfort zone, you might still be visited by the largeness of responsibility. When this happens, zoom out to the big picture. Write down a list of the fruits responsibility bears in your life. Mine are: freedom of schedule, creative freedom over my business, deciding who and what come into my space at all times, setting an ambitious salary, designing my life out of my own desires, finding fulfillment in my day to day life, supporting me and my husband's life, the ability to exercise my abundant mindset versus my lack mindset, confidence that I can handle life.

Those fruits are pretty sweet and I am so grateful I get to taste them every single day. They are my reward of responsibility.

In order to relish in the rewards of responsibility, we get to define and view the role it plays in our lives.

Where are you taking on responsibility with your business?

1. _____
2. _____
3. _____

What are the fruits that those responsibilities bear over your life?

1. _____
2. _____
3. _____

What is one area of your life that you have mastered the art of responsibility?

As the responsibility increases and you move through different levels of your business, what once knocked you off your feet with terror will seem like a walk in the park. I hired my third employee last month and I did it with excitement and ease. I felt a full-body panic with nausea come over me one morning as I sat journaling. I knew that feeling. I had experienced her before. I looked up from my journal and smiled. I knew that I was about to hire someone. The full-body panic and nausea immediately subsided as I slipped into the routine of hiring that was backed by evidence that I could handle supporting women that I admire on my payroll. I welcomed the responsibility because I saw what the future would hold if I hired another team member to Scout's Agency. That future looked damn beautiful and I got to be responsible for claiming it.

So this is your note, your permission slip, your invitation: it is okay to be afraid of responsibility. That next level of responsibility will soon become your next comfort zone. Hold on with both hands because you were made for this.

The Lesson: When you are afraid of responsibilities, acknowledge the doubt, and understand it is preparing you to uplevel to what's next.

PRAY FOR YOUR
FAILURES TO
ILLUMINATE THE
PATH YOU ARE
MEANT TO WALK
DOWN.

Lesson #20:

Failure Is What Gets You Closer to Success

"The most joy in life can be found amongst progress. If we can start to think of each 'comeback' as an exciting practice instead of an embarrassing one - we will not only be better equipped for success, but we will begin to feel and understand life on another level."

-Chelsea Curtis, co-host of What We Said Podcast

When I look back at my career, I see numerous stepping stones that got me to the life that I have today running Scout's Agency, being the co-host of Okay Sis Podcast, and hosting SCOUT Podcast. I call them stepping stones, marathons I had to run to get to this block, or stitches I had to stitch to see this exact picture.

Other people would call them failures.

A list of my failures in no particular order: I could not make a viable business out of my magazine, my blog, or my first podcast - three separate business ideas that I implemented and executed upon. Each were moved on from, chalked up to a good experience as I carried the lessons I had cultivated within each on to my next thing.

But here is how the weave goes, the larger than life connector that proves nothing in your life is random: the magazine led me to becoming the Director of Operations for EntityMag.com which made me fall in love with digital media which made me start my own blog which made me fall in love with content creation which made me start my own podcast which made me pivot into Okay Sis which made me fall in love with the podcasting world which made me start Scout's Agency which made me get to a point in my life where I was ready to publish a book where I had an agency at my disposal to help market it.

Every step built upon every step and therefore in my book failures aren't charged with a shameful energy. They can be devastating - grieving the end of a business has a poignant depth to it - but failure is just that whisper on your shoulder that says, *"Wrong turn, let's go this way."* Similar to anxiety, it is just a messenger and a guide. It is here to serve your most expansive of realities.

When you start your business or are in the depths of it, there will be launches, events, products, and/or courses that you would not categorize in hindsight as successful. The thing you put out there in the market that you believe is going to be a home run won't sell. You'll expect one hundred people to show up to your event when only ten will make it. You'll put two thousand into creating a course and only make five hundred dollars back. You will offer a freebie that no one wants to sign up for.

These things are inevitable in business. Parts of your business won't hit the market the way you expected them to - and that is okay. With our Instagram feeds flooded with offerings like, *"How to have a six figure launch"* or *"We sold out in 24 hours!"* It can be hard not to expect large things off the bat and it can be hard not to compare ourselves once our plan doesn't come to that big six figure fruition.

Those big money launches are totally possible but what they don't say behind those successful posts is that those usually aren't their first or their second or their third go at it. We consistently forget, as a society, that the successes of an entrepreneur make up 2% of their daily life. We all want to be Sara Blakely, but we don't want to build Spanx.

I am here to tell you, in a tough-love, look at yourself in the mirror way, you have to want to build Spanx. You can't just want to be Sara Blakely. If the recognition comes at the end of the day, beautiful! But that is not why you are here. You are here because you like building beautiful, purposeful, and cool shit that enhances your day-to-day life, challenges your personal development, and aligns you closer with what you are here to do during this lifetime.

I don't want to be Sara Blakely. If that comes with the ride, amazing. But I know what I do want to do - I want to *build*.

And with building, comes failure. And with failure, comes a lot of emotional challenges.

I have cultivated a lot of preventative strength around failure so that when it does come knocking at my door, I pivot versus deconstruct. Like all things in entrepreneurship, I had to renegotiate my relationship to this ominous force and have come to look at it as the most important guiding sign in my business. When Mady and I had difficulty selling tickets to our live event, instead of asking questions like, *"Is our community actually not that strong? Why aren't they showing up for us? Are we frauds?"* I asked myself questions like, *"Is the $20 price tag too high for our community? Would they feel more comfortable spending $10 on a virtual event? Is everyone burnt out on Zoom events - are we too late in the pandemic to put one on? Would our community rather buy sweatshirts from us versus events since our podcast content is free every week? Where is the purchasing power of our community? How can we work to bring them what they do want from us?"*

Those are two very different narratives. The former deflates you into a pool of unworthiness while the ladder starts strategizing how to make our next offering more successful and of better service for our audience.

There will be those moments when you sell out of your product, when an investor comes knocking to fully fund your project, when you have a six-figure launch, when you get featured in Vogue, when you double your pricing and people line up to pay, when your Instagram followers keep growing and growing and growing.

That's the beauty of this all. Part of the game is the wild, overly exhilarating successes that move the needle and the other part is the failures that show you where to place the needle in the first place.

But how to reestablish your relationship with failure to look at it as a beautiful mentor instead of the swift deconstruction that we all fear?

Accept it is coming: Before it even arrives and before we even get into the game, accept that something you do in your business will not be a success. You will place expectations and predictions on something that will not come to fruition. It might be public or it might be in private. Either way, if you walk into the house knowing that something won't go as planned on a micro level or on a macro level, you can manage your expectations of what this is all about. Accept that failure is a part of every entrepreneur's journey and at some point or another, if it hasn't already, it will become a part of yours.

Know that failure has shaped every entrepreneur: Sophia Amoruso left NastyGal which went bankrupt because she accepted inflated investments and put a pressure on the business to grow at lightning speed. This failure led her to Girlboss, which became an international women's business platform and movement. Her experiences scaling a multi-million business only to fail when investors came along didn't break her but rather propelled her into her next business. Every entrepreneur has a story where things just didn't quite work out - from a product launch that sold poorly to stepping down from a company that was going bankrupt. Imagine how your next failure is going to shape you.

Have a growth mindset around failure: Remember how we talked about business being personal? Your business is personal because it is your life's work but if someone does not engage in your services or products it is not a reflection of your self-worth. When you're not selling tickets to your event, never ponder what that means for you as a human being; instead, always ponder what it means about the market. Use your situation as an opportunity to do some market research and find the sweet spot where supporting your community feels beneficial to them and to you.

Know that there is less attention on you than you think: When you are on the precipice of a failure, you often are worried about your reputation and what others will think of you. None of that matters, because they most likely won't remember that your course didn't sell (will they even know?) or that you had to shut down your brick and mortar shop to pivot to e-commerce. The center of your universe is not rotating around anyone else's real estate of thoughts. It is okay if others know things didn't work out. They will admire you for your next move, not shame you for your last.

I know that within failure is a lot of fear and heavy chaos about the future. I know that it evokes anxiety that does not stop. I know that failure on a large scale of having to shut down your business is a real loss that can only be experienced through grief. I know that the prospect of failure might make you hesitate to even begin.

I also know that you will survive failure if you treat it as an opportunity to pivot to not just build future success but a stronger business and more inspiring offering which in turn will benefit and enrich your personal life.

At the end of the day, thank failure for showing up. It stopped you then and there from continuing down a path that just wasn't working so that you could engage your energy towards the avenues that are waiting for you to shine in, embrace, and claim as your own.

Allow it to whisper into your ear, "Wrong way, find another path," and then blossom your vision into a future potential that is so much greater than the one currently at play.

I always pray for the failures to come quickly so that I can sit sweetly with success. Pray for your failures to illuminate the path you are meant to walk down.

The Lesson: You are never a failure if you learn from something that "didn't work" and use those teachings to add more color to your life.

179

THE KEY TO
SELF-WORTH IS
DIVERSIFYING
YOUR IDENTITY
AND ULTIMATELY
GETTING TO KNOW
THE YOU WHO
LIVES REGARDLESS
OF YOUR JOB
TITLE, INCOME,
RELATIONSHIP
STATUS, OR DAILY
ROUTINE.

Lesson #21:

Your Worth Is Not Tied To Your Revenue

"I was never good at math anyway."

-Diana Espir, Producer, Podcaster, & Beauty Enthusiast

I remember when my agency was the gatekeeper to my emotions. If I signed a client that day, I was happy. If an opportunity I was banking on didn't come through, I was anxious. If a client wanted to part ways unexpectedly, I would ruminate in self-doubt. If I received an angry email from a podcast host or writer, I would shrink out of fear. If I succeeded my revenue goals for the month, I was ecstatic. My internal temperature was dictated by the success of my agency. Any given moment could and would alter my energy—which was usually comprised of small setbacks or insignificant email exchanges that by the next day would be erased from both parties' minds.

This codependency on your business, if engaged with over a long period of time, will reduce your perceived worth to the health and success of your business. If the business isn't doing so well, you will likely perceive a drop in your self-worth versus moments when your business is on fire. Let's cut the umbilical cord now because in the beginning, especially the beginning, the excitement of starting can be overwhelming and take over your mind. However, as you start to experience the peaks and valleys of your business, we need you to not be hostage to those waves. We need you to be grounded, clear, and ready for the next level. We need you to live within the truth that you are creating something far bigger than the setback or win of the day.

Equating one's self-worth with your career is something that is rapidly taking over millennials' mental health. The glorified aspects of our identity are often tied to work: who raised capital from whom, who won Forbes 30 Under 30, who got their product to a celebrity, who sold their company to Google, whose business Instagram hit 10k, and so forth.

We tie our self-worth to two cognitive machines within our business: the small daily ebbs and flows and the large milestone. There are two types of women: one who is hung up in the micro and one who is hung up in the macro.

Let's start with the macro woman.

I know so many close friends of mine who don't feel as if they have made it because they are not a public figure entrepreneur like Emily Weiss or Jen Atkin. They haven't had publicity coverage and aren't making the podcast rounds. They bootstrapped their business with no venture capital and their product isn't being seen yet by the top influencers or celebrities. Therefore, they think they haven't made it and then intrinsically take this metric of success and attach it to their self-worth. This type of woman who believes her self-worth lives in the macro is in danger of never enjoying the fruits of her labor along with the daily, smaller wins. Even if she hits a quarter of a million dollars in revenue or grows her business by 100% in her second year, she will be unable to celebrate or see the progress and the impressive successes she has achieved because she is chasing entrepreneurial fame or a specific metric of success like selling your company to Google or being a keynote speaker at Create & Cultivate.

This type of woman sets goals and then when she achieves them, they suddenly aren't as great as the next level. Her cup is never full because she is existentially seeking the destination, assuming that once she gets there, she will be happy, fulfilled, and satisfied.

The hunger never stops because destinations are fleeting moments and turn into future paths that are calling her name. She knows rationally that the destination is a facade and never exists but has difficulty integrating that truth on an emotional level. Under this principle, her self-worth will never come to fruition and she will never meet it because the destination will continue to develop and she will continue to chase it, hanging her self-worth on an external pin in the map that keeps traveling farther and farther away from her.

Resonating? Here are practices you can implement today to help overcome this destination seeking syndrome and start to enjoy the ride more:

- When a win happens within your business, pause imme-diately, take a deep breath, and put a smile on your face. Exercise the three small wins steps outlined in Lesson #18.
- Have a list of all of your successes handy on a Post-It note on your desk or on an even grander scale like a white board. Constantly refer back to everything you have achieved in moments where you feel small.
- Create a celebratory ritual with your team (or just your-self!) that when something does go right in your business, you celebrate in some way, whether that is sending a GIF to your Slack channel or texting your best friend to let them in on the good news!
- Unfollow every woman on social media who enables you to compare yourself to their success. These might be your friends (in which case, just mute them) but it is important that as you focus on rising your self-worth in the day-to-day and opening your eyes to the actual health and success of your business and of you, we need no distractions.

The second type of woman ties her self-worth to the daily, more subtle energetic flows of her business. She is the woman who flies high when she signs a client only to be drenched in anxiety when she gets an email from an unsatisfied customer who wants their money back two hours later. When her monthly revenue is rising, she feels confident and settled. When her monthly revenue dips, she feels shaky and insecure. The flow of the business is holding her emotions captive and she is giving her happiness, peace of mind, and confidence away to the external systems of her work. She is terrified of failure because if her self-worth is tied up in the specific daily health of her business, what would failure do to her emotional state?

Her life is a constant state of highs and lows. She is not able to find a stabilizing middle ground within her that has nothing to do with the external circumstances that play around her. She outsources her mood to her customers, clients, vendors, or manufacturers instead of finding her truth within.

Are you in the micro self-worth loop? Here are a few practices to help stabilize your daily mood:

- Do not start your day with work. Put your phone away for the first hour of your day and enjoy your coffee, journal, read, or take a walk with your dog. Make sure you have a moment to yourself that has nothing to do with your business.
- Find a breathing technique or a type of meditation that works for you. In moments where you find your levels rising high or dropping down low, pause what you are doing, walk outside, and breathe for a few minutes.
- And just like the macro self-worth woman, you also need a list of things you have accomplished handy for moments where your mood does get dark. Revisit this list when your mood is dipping.
- When something brings you down, ask yourself: Will this matter in 5 seconds? Will this matter in 5 minutes? In 5 hours? In 5 days? In 5 weeks? In 5 months? In 5 years? Stop when you feel the anxiety subside.
- Be excited about the wins your business brings you every single day but make sure you breathe through the celebration so as to not get manic or increasingly high. Feel the win but manage your nervous system with deep breathing as to not overwork it and burn it out on mania.

I resonate most strongly with the micro self-worth woman, the one who chalks up her self-worth to the current health of her business. Whichever woman you identify with, it can be increasingly difficult to not put societal pressure on ourselves when it comes to the success of our careers. The tips listed above for the micro or macro type of woman are excellent for starting to see the big-picture, rooting yourself in the current moment, and work on grounding the level at which your self-worth lives. However, that is not the entire picture. When it comes to self-worth, that inner journey is the one that far supersedes our businesses if we have the emotional awareness and bravery to see past the identities of our lives.

When I first started my agency, I threw my whole life into it. Everything I did on a daily basis was in support of Scout's Agency. I went through the stereotypical entrepreneurial experience: sacrificing my social life and sometimes even the health of my marriage to put my nose down and dig deep into my work at all times. It started with passion and enthusiasm—I couldn't wait to dig in. Scout's Agency was what I thought about the moment I woke up and the moment I went to bed—a true entrepreneurial love affair. I believe that in order to successfully launch something, you need a bit of this obsession and tunnel vision in the beginning. It is when you can't poke your head out of the hole and discover the rest of your life as your business begins to run that things get a bit murky.

When we put all of our energy into our businesses at the expense of other areas of our lives—our social life, our relationships, our family life, or our health—we put all of our identity eggs into one basket. I believe the key to self-worth is to diversify your identity and ultimately get to know the *you* who lives despite your job title, income, relationship status, or daily routine.

Your business is part of your identity but it is not the only one, nor is it always the most important. If your self-worth comes from your business, your self-worth is not built on a strong foundation because failure in entrepreneurship is a big potential outcome. If your self-worth is tied to something outside of you, how true is it?

It is easy to get swept up in the intricacies of your business and by all means, enjoy the highs and work through the lows, but something within you has to shine brighter than your Shopify account or the amount of followers you gained that week. You have to discover your self-worth within. In doing so, all of the outside noise will continue to chaotically dance around you but you will be impenetrable, or at least things won't take you out for long periods of time and with swift severity. You will have a foundation that you built yourself that is based upon the fact that you simply exist, that you are alive, and that you are worthy of just being here on this earth, standing and breathing. Build up your root chakra so your solar plexus chakra can shine.

Discovering your self-worth is a lifelong journey and one that is not as simplistic as I am perhaps making it out to seem here. While finding your self-worth is an entire book in itself, I do want to ignite the process for you here and now with a few tips.

A few ways to cultivate self-worth:

- *Do the things you love.* List out all of the things you love to do that bring you joy that do not bring you revenue or push you further along in your career. This could be reading, taking walks with a loved one, knitting, cooking, or dancing. Make sure every day you ignite one of these activities, if only for five minutes, and truly feel what it is like to do something simply just for pleasure.
- *Carve out alone time.* In a day of endless stimulus, text messages, emails, calls, and Instagram notifications, we can sometimes be physically alone working all day but energetically are swamped with countless outside energies. Alone time is sans phone preferably outside—a bath will work too. Again, this can be five minutes of just walking outside and staring up at the sky. It can be getting into a bath with your phone in the other room so all you have to do is sit there, soaking your body in the hot water. Make sure you get in touch with the energy that is just yours by stepping away from the stimulus of your life for just a few moments a day.
- *Journal.* I journal every single morning. It is the first thing I

- do after I pour my coffee and take my dog out. Journaling as a daily or consistent practice allows you to meet yourself, to live within the subconscious mind of what makes you you. I suggest writing without a journal prompt and just letting whatever comes to the page come without judgment or force. If you implement this practice daily, over time you will come home to yourself and meet your unique essence.
- *Seek therapy.* I am a huge proponent of therapy and not just because I have been in it since I was fourteen years old. Talking out your life with a therapist and carving out an hour a week to just focus on you will help you get closer and closer and closer to yourself. It will allow you to deal with your anxieties and fears head on before they fester for too long and it will illuminate behavioral connections you didn't even know were there.
- *I love you.* Say it to yourself every single day. Give yourself a hug and utter the three words we remind everyone else in our lives that we are close to but so often forget to say it to ourselves. Every morning, take a deep breath, put your arms around yourself, and say, "I love you."

There are so many other tools and practices that can get you closer to your self-worth but these right here are some of my favorite. As you move through getting to know yourself, your days will be less captive to the cascading mountains of your inbox. In return, you will be able to work on your business from a place of fulfillment where you feel grounded. It doesn't mean you won't ever be knocked off your balance, it just means you can come back home to yourself in those instances and get back on the saddle with a clear mind, poignant vision, and self-worth levels that blind the opposition.

The Lesson: External metrics have nothing to do with the internal progress and fulfillment you will live with on a daily basis.

YOU NEED TO
REPLENISH YOUR
BODY WITH SOME
DEEP SOULFUL
REST. YOU NEED
TO FILL THE WELL
WITH WATER THAT
IS NUTRIENT DENSE
AND WARM.

Lesson #22:

Rest Every Day And Often

"The most important lesson I've learned in life is to rest. My rest benefits every single area of my life- my work, my relationships, my confidence, my well being. Rest to me is different than being lazy. It's about intentionally doing what refuels me."

-Kenzie Elizabeth, Lifestyle Influencer & Podcaster

I feel it slowly spreading throughout my mind and body—a tedious yet physically altering warning sign: I am getting tired, my thought processes are worn out, and the clarity I enjoy working with is starting to fade. In short, I need to rest.

In today's hustle culture, the amount of hours we sleep versus the amount of hours we spend working is a very clear equation: less sleep, more work. The founder stories of consistently running on very little sleep to achieve grand success has infiltrated the narrative of what it means to be an entrepreneur. Hustle culture can confuse the average millennial into believing that their worth is tied up to the number of hours they put in and that an intensely productive day is a sign of career worth.

I prescribe to hustle culture for one of its main tenants: that to have a successful business, you have to roll up your sleeves and get to work, that it is not the same type of work as the traditional nine-to-five, that sometimes evenings and weekends are spent in your inbox or shipping out product, that there will be moments when you are supposed to be off the clock but duty calls, that you have to know you aren't entering into the glamour but into the scrappy, that you are willing to do what it takes to get your vision off the ground.

I have always been very vocal on the type of work it truly takes to run a successful business and how a lot of that work is what most people don't actually want to see through. I hustle because my business excites me so much, I wake up with an energetic pull to feed it. Everyday, I want to work. I love the idea of acquiring wealth, but I love the idea of earning it even more. My financial planner preaches the importance of feeding my retirement fund (which I do) but I tell him I will probably never retire. The hustle runs through my blood and in my veins. And if you aren't there yet, it will come. When you start your own thing, it begins to carry you with it like a strong one-sided tug-of-war toward your dreams.

What I do not prescribe to within hustle culture—and busy culture while we are at it—is the notion that rest is the thing that must be compromised to be a successful entrepreneur, or a successful anything for that matter. And while yes, I am talking about physical sleep, of which I get 8-9 hours every single night no matter what, I am also talking about deep, effective, and purposeful resting.

As you walk deeper into the garden of your business, you will find that it is more difficult to "turn off" once you have physically closed your laptop for the day. You will also find that the energy in which you output during the workweek is of more intensity due to excitement, passion, and potential anxiety. You are not passively working, just trying to fill an hourly quota. You are actively engaged because this is *your* baby.

In order to preserve that level of energetic intensity you will be living within during working hours, you need to replenish your body with some deep soulful rest. You need to fill the well with water that is nutrient dense and warm. You need to remove the constant stimulation from your nervous system and give it space to unwind and play gently. You need to give yourself time to just be with you.

Once you begin to take rest seriously in your day-to-day life, you'll recognize that sitting on the couch and binge watching *The Office* while texting your friends back and scrolling through Instagram is not actual rest. That is zoning out. That is numbing out. That is checking out. That does nothing to feed your soul. It serves a real purpose in your life. There are times when you want to unplug, disconnect from work, from being so highly attuned to your soul and the needs of your highest self. I hear you and I feel that frequently. I am not here preaching to never have a Netflix binge again or that you shouldn't spend your weekday evenings watching your favorite show—I do it all the time. I am here to reframe your idea of what resting every day means and not to get it confused with loafing for the sake of de-stressing. With this reframe, you can actively nourish your soul through purposeful restful activities so that you are energized to get to work the next morning.

Nourishing and rejuvenating rest, the type that will fuel your soul and keep you grounded every single day, is time to yourself without your phone or any type of screen. For me, I get into bed 30 minutes to one hour every single night before my bedtime and curl up with a good book. I walk outside without shoes, place my heels in the grass, and just look up at the sky for a few moments. I write in my journal. I cook a nourishing meal. I spend fifteen minutes moving my body in fluid dance moves just for the sake of intuitively feeling into that movement. I put on a face mask, make tea, and chat with my husband on the couch. I stop what I am doing in the middle of the day, close my eyes, and inhale some essential oils through six deep belly breaths. I go for a leisurely walk. I pray.

This is the type of rest that will keep you from burning out or overexerting your energy, which starts out of excitement and can become anxiety-induced workaholism if not checked. If you are a Google Cal girl like me where your days are color coded by the hour, add in nourishing rest time. Treat it like any other non-negotiable of your day: your Pilates session, your skincare routine, your work hours, and your rest moments. If you are more of a go-with-the-flow type of woman, check in with yourself every few hours and ask if you would benefit from alone time, or five minutes of purposeful rest.

Yesterday, I had four sales calls, one podcast recording, and one call with a vendor. To get through all the calls and presenting my best energy, I overamped my nervous system. I let the mania of the excitement overtake me. I enjoyed all of my calls and was looking forward to every single one of them, but when four o'clock hit and I could barely read my emails and my brain felt fuzzy, I realized I hadn't incorporated just five minutes of rest into my day to break up the back-to-back energy of connecting with others. Without that meaningful rest, I was operating on adrenaline and began to enter mania. And when you go up like that and are operating from high intensity energy, you *will* crash. And when you do crash, the rest of your day is shot and your productivity declines significantly.

In the perfect world, I would have stepped outside between every second call without my phone and stared at the sky, taking a few deep breaths for five minutes. I would have paused to journal. I would have said hello to my soul while asking her what she needs. I would have grounded myself with a quick five-minute meditation. And then, come four o'clock, I would have been in a much better state of mind to clear out my inbox and end on a high note.

I was talking to a family member about work and telling him all about running Scout's Agency, growing Okay Sis podcast, and writing this book. He asked me how many hours a week I was working—assuming the number was astronomical. To be honest, I don't know how many hours a week I work, although I can bet it is probably around the average 40-50 hour work week. I stopped measuring my days by the numbers of hours in my work week and started seeing them as the quality of hours I played within. One can work a ten-hour day but truly only get three hours of uninterrupted, productive work done. One person's hour of work can be someone else's three hours. It is the reason I hate hourly rates. When I can optimize my energy by taking care of myself with eight to nine hours of physical sleep, a focused and connected morning routine, nutritious meals, thirty minutes of exercise, fulfilling rest moments throughout the day, and ending the day with connecting inward, not zoning out to the endless feed of social media, I can operate out of clear and eager energy during my work hours. Five hours of truly in the flow work is better than eight where your mind is wandering or you keep reaching for coffee or you are texting your friend back in between emails. I am purposeful with my hours and when I am working, I am working and when I am resting, I am resting. I value each equally because working is not as enjoyable without the resting. Your soul has to light up to flow through with your dreams.

If you want to optimize your hourly work so that you have more time to get creative with no end goal or have more movie nights with your significant other or have the ability to create more moments to simply just be, then the rituals and habits in which you take care of yourself on a daily basis are key. I would rather work seven hours a day and have those seven hours be intentional and productive than ten hours a day and feel as if I am going nowhere fast, lost in a sea of to-do lists and multitasking objectives.

The first step to being really present at work is taking inventory of where you allot your time. It starts with checking your screen time metrics and taking an honest look at how many minutes (or hours!) you spend on social media apps like Instagram and Tik-Tok. I created the time inventory guide here to help you illuminate the areas you can discard and implement the activities that feed your soul.

Time Inventory:

How many hours a day do I spend on social media apps?

How do I feel after I go down a rabbit hole scrolling on social media?

How many hours on average do I spend watching TV during the week?

How do I feel about that number?

List the activities that I engage with on a daily basis that do not make me feel fulfilled or inspired:

1. _____
2. _____
3. _____

     a. Total hours per week: _____

What are three activities that make me feel good in my soul?

1. _____
2. _____
3. _____

What would my life look like if I swapped out half of the hours I spend on social media, watching TV, and engaging in activities that do not fulfill me with those three activities that make me feel good in my soul?

Would I feel more rested and centered? _____

Would I feel more refreshed to work when it is work time?

_____

Would I feel more connected to myself? _____

If you answered yes for the last three questions, then you have your resting answer! The answer for dealing with unwinding from a stressful workload is not to detach and numb yourself away from your body and your present moment. The answer is to engage in activities that ground and fill you up.

Yes, resting is getting enough sleep and watching a TV show or two after work. It is also consciously making the decision to use your rest time to fill up your soul and nourish your heart. That nourishment will help you wake up the next morning refreshed, rejuvenated, and inspired.

Your state of mind and energy levels are going to be essential as you grow, build, and operate your business. Protect them at all costs by infusing moments of soul-filled rest into your day. Nourish yourself so you can nourish your business.

The Lesson: Resting is as productive as hustling.

BELIEVING IN YOURSELF MEANS THAT THE ONLY PERSON YOU REPORT TO IS YOU.

Lesson #23:

Actually Believe In Yourself

"One of the most important lessons I learned early on is to not be afraid to put yourself out there. Don't be afraid that people won't like you. Being 100% yourself is your most valuable asset and it's important to not let anyone tell you otherwise. Follow your dreams fearlessly, listen to your heart, and focus on doing the things that make you feel good. Being unequivocally yourself will help you find your people and your path. Be confident in your convictions and don't second guess your intuition."

-Shani Darden, Esthetician and Founder of Shani Darden Skin Care

I can guarantee that at one point or another in the beginning of your entrepreneurial journey where your business is more in ideation mode or perhaps in early execution, you will hear hesitant concerns from someone you love.

I have heard them plenty of times: *It's a little early to quit your day job, don't you think? Do you have time to start an agency? You have a really nice paying job, why would you risk it to start your own thing?*

In these initial stages, you will be buzzing from energy and in love with your future dreams. You will approach your spouse, parent, best friend, or sibling with such passion that you are certain they will not only be excited for you, but also ridiculously supportive. As your business plan spills out of your mouth with an animated face and your hands dancing in the space around you, you will expect a matching expression of excitement. And you might get that. But other times, that face staring back at you—the one you have grown up with, love, is a part of your family, or is your family— will project one back of worry, fear, and a brutal need to protect.

You will hear things like: *Are you sure you want to leave your cushy job where you are making a good stable income? How are you going to make any money with that? Do you even have time for this? You're putting your savings into this? But you're on such a great track at the law firm! Why would you want to mess that up?*

I have heard them over and over and over again. Sometimes from my spouse, sometimes from my dad, sometimes from a friend. And when I hear that question of concern, I know in my heart that I am onto something.

When you hear a loved one express worry over your new dream decisions, it is because of this one very simple idea: They live in the box that almost guarantees to bear them fruit. You are going to exit that box where there are less guarantees and more responsibility to bear your own results. They are concerned on a survival level that if you leave the box, you won't have any fruit to eat.

In other words, they are trying to protect you: from failure, from being in debt, from slim finances, from disrupting the trajectory of your career, from not having enough money to live your life. They are trying to keep you safe.

In those moments, where our loved ones are offering a blanket of safety over our shoulders if we just stay put, we have to look within and remember why we are doing what we are doing. We didn't come here to play safe. We didn't come here to play small. We are entrepreneurs because if we don't get out the idea that lives in our head, we will emotionally and mentally go crazy. We are entrepreneurs because building something out of the vision that gets projected within our minds is the only path forward. We are entrepreneurs because that box we grew up in doesn't work for us. And while that box lights so many people up and drives them toward fulfillment, we just simply need a new one.

And so, we take risks and we create our own businesses.

But if you don't believe in yourself, you won't get through test number one: the concerned and doubting loved one.

So here is your warning: this test will come to you and your answer either exhibits your belief in yourself or your ability to easily crumble in the presence of someone else's opinion.

If you are having trouble believing in yourself, don't worry. It's a muscle that needs to be worked and is not inherent within us by the time we have gone through life's loops. Ed Mylett always says that self-confidence comes when we keep the promises we make to ourselves. There is something wildly simplistic yet profound in that idea.

Let's talk about upping that self-confidence, which will in return grow the muscle of believing in yourself. First, let's look at the evidence of areas in your life that you have delivered on the promises you made for yourself. These could range from *I promised myself that I would stick* to *my skincare routine every night and I have for the past two months* to *I promised myself that I would blog every single day about my wedding planning process* to *I promised myself that I would put my phone away every single night at 8:30 pm.* Let's collect the evidence that you do, in fact, keep promises to yourself. And once the evidence is collected, free journal about how those kept promises make you feel.

Promises I kept to myself:

   1. _____

   2. _____

   3. _____

How I feel knowing that I kept those promises to myself:

Since believing in yourself and your competency is a muscle, let's set some new promises to grow and grow and grow that inner assurance that when you make a promise to yourself, you keep it.

New promises I am making to myself:

   1. _____

   2. _____

   3. _____

How I will feel once I keep these promises to myself:

Now we have logged evidence of areas that you have delivered and shown up for yourself, where you have changed habits or up-leveled in an area of your life. Even better, you have new promises you are excited to keep because you know that keeping the promises you make to yourself is the number one way to move through life with confidence and with action.

But that doesn't mean that your loved ones won't try to keep you from living your dream. They will try to keep you in the arena that is technically working for you: stable income, benefits, a directional career. They will try to keep you from taking executive ownership over your life because they too are afraid of the uncertainty of that outcome.

When you have decided in your soul that you are going for it, you'll need to keep that decision safe within so that it is impenetrable from outside forces while also pulling at that inner belief in yourself. To keep that decision safe, there are two things you can do:

1.) *Feel your decision.* Before telling anyone about your new venture, feel what it feels like to be excited about it. Observe how in alignment it is for your soul. Take a few moments to yourself to access this energy and imagine it rising like a brick wall around you, keeping you safe from those that are trying to keep you in your comfort zone. Imagine your decision sprouting roots from your feed into the ground, harnessing itself into the depths of the earth.

2.) *Identify what is fear and what is valuable feedback.* When you get news that is anything but favorable toward your new venture, you get to identify which aspect of that feedback is fear-based and which aspect of that feedback is actually really great insight that you can take and use to become stronger in your business. Remember: not all criticism is something you should turn your back from but identifying which can help and which is a projection of their own shit is key here.

- Fear-based feedback: You just got a raise at your job. Don't you think it's foolish to give that up?
- Valuable feedback: You just got a raise at your job. Start putting that raise into savings so that you are in a good situation if you do decide to go full time on this venture.

See the difference there? Always try to decipher when someone is projecting their fears onto you or when they are trying to be realistic and help. This will help you know when to discard feedback, stay in your lane, and up the belief in yourself or when to really listen and absorb knowledge.

1. *Scan yourself for the answers:* A lot of times, especially those who are empaths, we take on others' opinions, emotions, and energies. If someone is projecting fear at us, we might adopt that fear as our own and confuse ourselves with that fear. When someone tells you you can't do it or that you should reconsider, scan your body for what is your emotional frequency and what is theirs. Yes, you will harbor a certain amount of fear as you move forward in your business, but is it the healthy fear that is expansive and moving you forward or are you adopting the fear of others that is limiting and self-sabotaging? Always scan your emotional state and recognize what is yours and what is theirs.

Believing in yourself is staying in your own lane. It is putting blinders on and following what feels good for you. It is not disregarding fear or practical advice from others who are wiser than yourself. It is about being able to select which advice and opinion you take on energetically and emotionally and which you get to discard because it doesn't fit with your bottom line soul mission.

Believing in yourself means hearing other's opinions and sticking true to the one that is your path. It is being your biggest advocate when you might have doubters and naysayers. It is understanding the emotional reasoning behind why your loved ones are asking you to proceed with caution. It is knowing—and I have said it before!—that no matter what, you got this. You walk into a room with your head held high. You wake up each morning to create exactly the type of life you yearn for in your heart. You allow others fears to be heard but never to be considered. You listen to outside opinions and take what works for you and discard what doesn't with a ruthless force. Believing in yourself means that you are ready to jump through the tests, pass the self-doubt, be unfazed by the external critique, and do what you want to do. At all times. Throughout your career. And within your business. Believing in yourself means that the only person you report to is you.

You have to find that inner creative force that pulls you toward the life of your dreams. You have to be your biggest fan. You have to show up for the version of yourself that is scared and begging to stay in her comfort zone. You have to believe in yourself, whole-heartedly in a ride-or-die kind of way. You have to believe in you.

The Lesson: Be your biggest fan when everyone else is projecting their fears onto you.

FIND THE YOU IN THERE THAT EXISTS REGARDLESS OF ALL OF YOUR EXTERNAL LABELS AND REVERE HER AS HOLY, BEAUTIFUL, AND POWERFUL.

Lesson #24:

Love Yourself And Then Love Yourself Some More

"Putting yourself first is key. When I started DedCool in 2016, the 100+ hour weeks seemed to be the only feasible way of getting my company off the ground. In 2018, I started to look at things through a new perspective (due to a decline in my physical and mental health). As I grew the business while also growing as an individual, I now understand the importance of self-care. When burn out happens (it will happen), quality of life and quality of will show to be unforgiving. Take care of yourself and always make sure to love yourself some more."

-Carina Chaz, Founder and CEO of DedCool

I remember the secretive and blood-thumping-through-my-veins moment. I was in my office on Zoom with the three ladies who were in the mastermind I was a member of. The mastermind was for women in their first six months of business who also valued and lived a spiritual life. Our facilitator, who is now my mindset coach, had given us journal prompts based upon the guest speaker of the week, which was all around our social media presence. So the four of us decided to do them together over Zoom.

We went through each of the prompts, spent time in reflection writing our answers, and then shared with one another our findings. As intuitive women, we were open to exploring what our subconscious had to say around things like the fear of putting oneself out there or the truth about our finances. It was, as they say, a safe space.

We got to one prompt, which stopped me in my tracks: *What would you share online if you weren't afraid?*

At that point, I had detailed my journey of living with bipolar disorder. I had openly and candidly talked about being hospitalized, self-harming as a teenager, being on a slew of medication, going through two outpatient programs, psychosis, and my suicidal ideation. I had thought, up until that moment, that I had talked about it all—the shocking, the taboo, and the personal.

But something else came through and my entire body got hot and I started sweating. My team was in the room, and while I had spoken the other answers out loud for them to hear, this one I wanted to keep within my mastermind container.

When it got to my turn to share, I typed it into the chat because I wasn't ready to declare it out loud.

I wrote: *If I wasn't afraid, I would share that I love myself. I love myself so completely. I just am absolutely in love with being me.*

In a sea of women being stifled from self-doubt, imposter syndrome, and encouraged humility, I recognized in that moment why this was such a difficult thing for me to claim out loud. In today's society, we are marketed to love ourselves, but no one tells us what to do when that actually comes true.

And fear kicks in. Will I sound arrogant? Or full of myself? Or worse—narcissistic?

We are encouraged to love ourselves, to practice self-love through skincare and long walks, through journaling and meditation, through carving out time for just ourselves in our day. But then when we actually get there? When we actually feel like standing at the mountain top and profess our love for ourselves? We cower and play small so as to not offend or be judged. We were tricked into thinking it is the forever pursuit of loving ourselves versus the actual presence of loving.

So, I am here to give you the biggest permission slip of your life: You can love yourself and you can show up loving yourself in whatever room you find yourself in or at whatever table you make a seat for yourself at. You get to occupy space and have that space be unconditional love for who you are in any given moment. You get to not just be on the self-love journey, but embody it. You get to love yourself.

We are all on different detours on the journey and if you're sitting here shaming yourself for not being further along, my darling, that doesn't matter. I too fall out of alignment and self-destructive thoughts enter my mind that are anything but loving. I too need to remind myself of how much I do love myself and recenter into that vibration. It isn't about where you drift off to, but about how you get back onto the path.

Here are some ways I pump self-love through my veins because just like your relationship with a significant other, friend, or family member, you have to put in the work.

How to Stop Comparing & Cheer Women On Instead

I could go on and on about how social media, specifically Insta-gram, has created an entire culture of comparing women's high-light reels to our low points. We scroll through our feed and see someone in a perfect house, with a perfect family, and perfect hair, skin, body, job, book deal, Forbes feature, insert anything and ev-erything here. And then, we diminish our lives, our successes, our accomplishments, and the blessings in our lives because of our in-ability to see the beauty we do have within this square of perfectly edited and perfectly curated imagery.

I know that comparing yourself to other women on the internet or other female entrepreneurs can stop you dead in your tracks and make you feel less than, maybe even paralyzed out of taking action. There is always the option to unfollow if someone is mak-ing you feel such envy to the point of low self-worth, but there is something to be said about the fact that this is just our go-to behav-ior these days: compare yourself to a woman's highlight reel and then beat yourself up for not having what she has. So, instead of unfollowing everyone who could inspire you if given the chance, run through these three quick mindset shifts every time you see a woman on social media that you compare yourself to:

1. *Cheer her on.* When you start comparing, stop yourself and take a breath. Then, instead of being jealous of what she has, send her a congratulations! Comment that you are happy for her. Send her love and joy and a prayer that her success only multiples from here on out.

2. *Identify the areas that this woman can serve as an inspiration for you.* Is it clear that you need to make a plan to save for your dream home? Is it time to start thinking about starting a fam-ily? Is it the emotional pull you need to take your career into your own hands and get creative with your entrepreneurial

future? Whatever it is you are envious of her for, turn within and ask how you can use this as inspiration to create systems and strategies to make that a reality in your own life.

3. *Realize another woman's accomplishments don't take away from your pot.* Present to your mind the mindset shift that her having the million dollar business or her being a guest on your favorite podcast has nothing to do nor has any impact on whether or not you can stand in that exact same position one day. A woman having something we want does not mean that she took the last bite of ice cream. It means she opened the jar for us all.

4. *Identify three things you feel really grateful for and three things you have accomplished that you are proud of.* Remember to tap back into the big picture of your life because it is fruitful.

I have never had a crippling problem with comparing myself to other women like I know many others live with. Overall, I have always recognized that their lane doesn't change or diminish mine. However, I am human and it happens. I remember stumbling upon this woman's Instagram I did not know—I think she lived in Australia—and her caption on one of her photos was a breakdown of how much money she made that month. At the bottom, the total stood there staring back at me: $80,000. One month. $80,000.

My first reaction was extreme and utter jealousy, and a little bit of anger if we are being honest. I wanted that and I wanted that now. And the thoughts began: How could she pull that off? I could never pull that off. That is a unicorn situation. That isn't available to the rest of us.

And then, I kept reading. She posed a question at the end of her caption. She called out the fact that there will be two types of women who read this: the first type is extremely jealous, looking at what they have in comparison with a large deficit, and is judging her as bragging and being boastful. The other type is cheering her on, proud of her, and expanding their monthly revenue goals in their own mind.

Which type of woman do you want to be? I am committed to living as the latter because committing to living as the latter will not only send love their way, but it will also strengthen and deepen the love you have for yourself.

Spend Time Alone With Just You

I found that the more I enjoyed spending time alone with just me, the more I grew to love myself. As an entrepreneur and truly as anyone who is alive on this planet, we are living within a conversation that exists between us and everyone else, including our significant others, best friends, parents, siblings, clients, employees, peers, mentors, professional network, kids...it goes on and on. We also live in a conversation that exists between our soul and our mind: a never-ending thought loop that creates ideas but that also creates fears.

In order to love ourselves, we have to omit the noise and feel what it feels like to just be with ourselves.

I am not asking you to develop an incredibly long meditation practice, because I don't do that myself, or find a way to rid the thoughts in your mind for a certain period of time each day. What I am asking is that you go outside without your phone and just sit on a chair for five to ten minutes. That you take some time to close your eyes and take six deep breaths. That you take a bath without a book or a podcast playing, just a candle lit and some sage. That you pause to just be you—you without the job title, you without the family title, you without the responsibilities.

Some of my favorite ways to spend time with myself:

Take myself on a date: Call up a restaurant, make a reservation for one, plan a fancy outfit, do your hair and makeup, take an Uber, order a glass of wine, and treat yourself to a nice meal with just yourself.

Take a bath: But don't just take a bath. Take a bath without your phone, a book, a podcast playing, music, or any external content playing. Dim the lights, light a candle, and just soak in the hot water.

Journal: Spend some time journaling every single day. Carving out journaling time will allow you to deeply connect with yourself.

Do a gentle workout: Sometimes, when I need to just be with me and my body, I do a 20-minute Pilates workout in my backyard. The phone gets put away and I get to just focus on my body.

Have a solo dance party: Put on your favorite song and dance alone like a crazy, full of life, passionate woman.

Pull cards: If you need help tapping in, pull a card to help guide you. I recommend The Inner Compass deck.

Engage in a hobby: Spend time painting, writing poetry, or gardening without any expectation of return.

Find the you in there that exists regardless of all of your external labels and revere her as holy, beautiful, and powerful. Visit her often and send her love. Pause and just be with you.

Feeling Proud Of Yourself

I believe that, as women, we have a divine duty and obligation to stand up and place our mark on the world, acknowledge where our zone of genius is, and exude that confidence as we dance through life.

Talking about our accomplishments or even identifying them yourself can be challenging and an uncomfortable process for so many. But, my love, life is too short to spend so much time validating your pain and so little time celebrating your accomplishments.

We often sit in conversations discussing our traumas and wanting to be seen for the hardships and challenges we have survived or are currently in survival mode around. This is one side of the spectrum of life—the painful, messy, and chaotic growth experiences. We must not forget the other spectrum of life—the beautiful triumphs, the creations, and the wins that you put into action.

To love yourself is to be proud of yourself for simply being alive but also for what you have done with this life. If you are reading this and thinking to yourself, "I haven't done anything noteworthy though," I am going to confidently tell you that it is a false limiting belief that is appearing as truth. Of course you have done something noteworthy. If you are living, you have done something noteworthy.

Let's get comfortable with expressing our pride because we are going to put pen to paper and look our accomplishments in the eye. We are going to hold this list close, so that in times of self-doubt or self-destruction, we can pull this list out and see concretely the inspiring things we have done.

As you create this list, please note each line does not need to be enormous accomplishments like: sold my company to Google or hit a six-figure revenue in my first year or graduated Harvard Business School. Definitely include your biggest wins but also make sure to infuse the more subtle achievements in too, such as: I decided to start my own business even though I live with high anxiety, or I made my first sale, or I was really supportive for a friend when she was going through a rough time, or I decided to invest in myself by hiring a business coach, or I drafted up a business plan.

Put as much as you want here—every little thing you have ever been proud of from career achievements to personal accolades. This is the moment you get to grab and internalize your greatness.

My Proud List:

1. _____
2. _____
3. _____
4. _____
5. _____

Repeat Your Positive Affirmations

When it comes to the art of loving ourselves, we oftentimes don't believe in the notion itself. This leads us to helplessly search for self-love but falling short. This is where the beauty of positive affirmations comes in. Landing on a positive affirmation that feels good to you and then repeating that affirmation over and over each day will allow the message of the affirmation to permeate into your soul. Eventually, after hearing it so many times and after saying it out loud repeatedly, you will begin to adopt it as your belief. There is power in claiming things out loud and we must always take the narrative we tell ourselves seriously.

Your positive affirmation doesn't have to be this grand manifesto. Start small. Affirmations such as: *I love myself, I am worthy of love, I am love, or I will always love myself are beautiful places to start.*

There are a few ways to help your positive affirmation start to settle into your belief system. For me, I always write the affirmation I am adopting onto a post-it note and paste it to my bathroom mirror so that as I am going through my skincare routine, my affirmation is staring me in the face.

Saying it out loud to yourself in the morning as you take three deep breaths and put one hand over your heart is another meaningful way to soak in the affirmation. Writing it in your journal over and over and over again daily is also an amazing practice.

The important thing here is the repetition. Hold your affirmation close and repeat it in your head, out loud, or on paper every time you need that reminder of your life for yourself.

Loving yourself is a lifelong path and one of the main purposes of our human existence. As with all things in life, it is a cyclical practice. There will be moments where you regress backwards and others where you leap forwards. However, as you embark on making your dreams come true and are tested with the emotions we cover in this book—fear, anxiety, and self-doubt—coming home to yourself and knowing you love you will help you persevere.

Your love for yourself will permeate out from within and into your business.

The Lesson: If you are going to build a life you love, you have to love yourself more deeply than you ever thought was possible.

SOMETIMES, IN THE DEPTHS OF OUR TO-DO LISTS, IN THE CONFINES OF OUR RESPONSIBILITIES, AND IN THE TRENCHES OF OUR INSECURITIES, WE FORGET. WE FORGET THE MOST PROFOUND LAW OF NATURE: LIFE IS BEYOND BEAUTIFUL.

Lesson #25:

Life Is Beyond Beautiful

"I'll never forget walking past a bank in Amsterdam in 2011 with a window display that said 'Life is full of beauty. Notice it.' It didn't seem like a monumental life moment at the time but it's something that has always stuck with me. You see, what we choose to focus on is what we experience more of in this lifetime. I spent a lot of my life focusing on the negative, the fears, the excuses but once I stepped back and acknowledged there was still so much to be grateful for, even in the hardest of days, my quality of life changed. So take time to appreciate every smile, cherish every hug, be present for every laugh and notice the beauty... because it is there if you look."

-Bailey Stanworth, Co-host of What Day Is It? Podcast and Founder of PLAY Digital

I was sitting outside in a courtyard alone surrounded by lush trees and guarding bushes. The spectrum of greens ranged from fluorescent lime to deep earthy tones. Birds were singing to one another as I saw a bunny hop across the outskirts. The soundtrack was the majestic and ease-filled flow of nature. I sat there feeling full and in awe of my surroundings. How strong the tree to the left of me had rooted itself up and up and up. How its leaves provide optimal shade and created a stain glass effect when the sun shone through at different points of the day. The wind made a slight appearance, gracing my cheeks. I looked around and let my surroundings seep into my soul. In that moment, I was consciously aware of the fact that life was and is so extremely beautiful.

Sometimes, however, in the depths of our to-do lists, in the confines of our responsibilities, and in the trenches of our insecurities, we forget. We forget the most profound law of nature: that life is beyond beautiful.

You are The Emotional Entrepreneur, therefore you are in tune with the subtleties of emotional shifts as well as the enormous tidal waves they can consume us with. You also know, even if you forget at times, that life exists despite your emotional landscape. That when you are feeling knee deep in overwhelm, the butterfly still flies outside and the sunset still paints a magical picture each night. That even when you think everything is crumbling around you, you still awake each morning with a new day and fresh breaths waiting to be taken. That even when you think you have made the most colossal mistake in your business, a happy client is waiting for you to acknowledge her success.

Life can get really tough, but you already know that. I believe our universal assignment as human beings on earth is to walk through challenging moments so that we can live the rest of our days with the unique wisdom-filled codes our pain fills us with, if we are so open to receiving them. What you might not emotionally recognize is that toughness, that pain, that heaviness is a universal human experience. We all get to walk through moments of hardship on both a small or large scale. It doesn't matter the weight in which it carries; what matters is that when we are leaning into hardship, we also hold the bigger picture that beauty is all around us and that life always offers inspiration if we so choose to see it, seek it, and claim it for ourselves.

I have experienced so many moments in my life while suffering within the shroud of my bipolar disorder where I said to myself, I cannot take this anymore. I cannot do it. The odd thing about that moment of giving up is that I continued to take it, I continued to bear it, and I continued to survive it because I had no choice. Every time I said I could not handle my emotions, I continued to handle them because emotions will visit you regardless of whether or not you want them or think you can handle them. Sometimes their visit is short, other times it is long. The difference between my foundational state now and then when emotional turmoil hits is simply that I now know that I am safe no matter what emotion I experience. This inherent belief in safety comes from the fact that I currently know that when depression or anxiety overtakes my system, beauty still exists outside of that singular, temporary experience.

Life also exists outside of your business, your career, and your passions. The waves will continue to crash and retract, regardless of your monthly revenue projections. The sun will rise and set regardless of your employee suddenly quitting. Your dog will still want snuggles at the end of the day even if you missed a deadline. And love, in any sort of capacity, will always be waiting for you when you temporarily leave it in pursuit of putting out a business fire.

It is easy to be in it, enveloped in the thick of things and laser focused on the micro happenings of your entrepreneurial career. As the leader of the ship, those details are important. As the leader of the ship, you must know the world revolves regardless of those details.

I know that this journey will not always be exciting or even feel fulfilling at times. Pursuing your passion is marketed to us as complete bliss 24/7 where alignment carries us through each second of our waking days. Pursuing your purpose guarantees only one thing: that when you go to bed at night, more often than not, you will feel fulfilled. It does not shield you from the ebbs and flows of life or the mind tricks your emotions will play on you. It only offers that through your navigation of life, you will possess a foundation that provides you with a deep sense of meaning. And at the end of the day, we may seek peace or happiness, but if our lives can hold a sense of meaning, we can endure whatever we need to to rise into the women we were destined to be.

Hold on knowing that this is the cyclical pattern of life and in moments where the cycle is not in your favor is the moment you get to show yourself how willing you are to hold on. It is the tough times that saturate the good times with that extra hint of color. It is the remembrance of the good times that will get you through the tough ones. It all serves one another—one beautiful dance between you, your dreams, and your soul.

Feel the emotional journey, the growth, and the hardships but always remembers what lies outside of you. Sometimes, entrepreneurship can feel so large to our self-centered viewpoint. At the end of the day, you could lose your company and still survive if you chose to. All of what we have here is temporary regardless of our name on the LLC or the receipt that confirms our purchase. So don't forget to dance. Don't forget to laugh. Don't forget the universal truth that life is beautiful.

You get to be here. You were chosen to live out this human experience and so you can't just love it conditionally, you get to love it unconditionally. That means embracing the painful moments. That means even when something doesn't go in your favor, you are grateful that you were placed into the position in the first place. As The Emotional Entrepreneur, you get to know that through pain comes growth. You can and will take on the hard shit in pursuit of your inner development. You get to taste the fruits of your labor because you chose the labor and the type of fruits you wanted to plant. There is nothing you cannot do if you so choose.

And so I am asking you here, humbly pleading and begging with you, to please choose the perspective that life is beautiful. To choose the perspective that you can ride the emotional waves presented to you with a deep, deep understanding that you are capable, safe, and ready to receive what this life has to offer you. To choose the you that holds the long-term vision, the you that shows up as her highest self, the you that is waiting for you to believe in her.

On days when the schedule is jam-packed, we are questioning our worth, self-doubt is creeping in, and our limiting beliefs surge to the surface, we must remember that life is holy and sacred and miraculous and beautiful. It is always there, offering itself to us, if we just shift our perspective to marvel and receive.

The Lesson: Regardless of the emotions that come up in any given moment, life is beautiful, and we have to be grateful we are given the chance to live it as emotional entrepreneurs.

ACKNOWLEDGEMENTS:

Where to begin when writing acknowledgements for a book that not only had the operational support to launch, but also years of emotional support so that I could get to the point where these lessons poured out of me?

I'll start with the source—my parents.

To my father, whose endless commitment to my mental health has been more than I could ask for. Thank you for being my foundation in moments when I could not hold myself. Thank you for being a guiding mentor whenever I enter new territories in my business. Thank you for loving me in all that I am, for seeing my essence, and for always supporting me—especially when times have been rough. I remember calling you crying as a freshman in college and hearing your confusion—Is there something bigger going on with my daughter, or is she just homesick? We explored that "something bigger" together as I entered into my diagnosis. Thank you for understanding, for researching when you didn't, and for always being one phone call away. I love you.

To my mother, who mirrored and saw the beauty in me before I could see it in myself. You always wanted an extraordinary life for me and were always there to hear me out when I needed to work through the intricacies of my emotional experience. While it took me a long time to understand this sentiment, you always reminded me that my depressive episodes would pass. In many ways, I believe I am a mirror image of you—or that at least, it in one lifetime, our souls were twins. Thank you for always understanding me—there is truly no aspect of my life I cannot go to you for. I am so aware that that kind of support is highly rare within a mother-daughter relationship, and I treasure it immensely. Thank you for teaching me how to be a woman.

To my sister, who I have spent the last 27 years of my life with but most importantly, who I have spent the last 3 years with having concentrated conversations about our self-worth, self-development, and our passions over at the Okay Sis podcast. Being your sister has been one of my highest honors. I cannot imagine how I could have gotten to this point without you and our hundreds of recorded episodes together. Thank you for growing up with me, for growing with me, and for uncovering the topics of life with me. Thank you for getting me out of my shell and teaching me that my silly, uncensored self is my true, authentic self.

To my grandparents, aunts, uncles, and cousins—my life is enriched because of you. I cannot fathom the luck I was granted the moment I was chosen to be born into this family. You are loud, flamboyant, full of life, supportive, and wise. To Grandma and Oma—you always saw such beauty in me, and I treasure all of our conversations over the years.

To my stepfather, Stephen, for giving me Natalia, Stephanie, and Aaron and for treating Mady and me as if we were your own. Your love for our family is endless, and I am so proud to not only know you, but to be your stepdaughter.

To all of my second mothers: Elizabeth, Sandi, and Deborah. Each one of you was put in my life during different unique phases, but something that you all have in common is the endless love you have given me. They say it takes a village, and you three have been an integral part of my village as second mothers. I am so blessed to have had Elizabeth and Sandi when I did and am eternally grateful that Deborah has been passed the baton.

To the Sobels, my in-laws, my chosen family: I am so proud to have joined your family and to be your family. I won the in-law jackpot when I married Adam and am always so grateful for your support and love. Mona and David, thank you for treating me like one of your own.

To my best friends—you know who you are. You have watched me ride this entire wave and have always been there for me in a way I cannot ever repay. I love you all. I feel understood because of you. I feel as if I will never be alone because of you.

To my coach, Amy Natalie, who made space for my emotional healing because she believed in and saw a version of me that I did not know was possible to embody. You have profoundly changed my life in the most impactful and important of ways. I am forever in gratitude and in debt for the container you have invited me into—the container of living my truth and the container of feeling confident in my emotional capacity to embody my life. Thank you, thank you, thank you for showing me how to fight for my life.

To my team at Scout's Agency for supporting the vision of amplifying female voices through podcasting. Thank you for believing in me, for showing up for the mission, and for supporting me in launching this book.

To the sisterhood—thank you for supporting Mady and my evolution with Okay Sis. I often find it so surreal that we have this community not only behind us, but with us. You are all more than I could have dreamed of. Being surrounded by a community of women who are willing to be vulnerable, resilient, and passionate while knowing the power of being silly and of good branding is the absolute best.

To the women quoted in this book—thank you for being in my circle. Thank you for supporting me in the many ways you have. Thank you for stepping up with your wisdom to show others what is possible when they follow their dreams.

To Jessica Zweig for writing the foreword of this book and for your beautiful validation of my story. Thank you for being not a client, not a friend, but a soul sister. I am so grateful Scout's Agency brought me to you.

To Rea Frey and the team at Writeway™—this book would not be what it is without your guidance. Thank you for believing in my message and helping me execute it to its full potential.

And lastly, and most importantly, to my husband. Thank you for inviting me into the world of healing. Thank you for believing in me and sticking through poignantly painful moments within my mental illness. Thank you for being so committed to our shared future vision. Thank you for allowing me to be silly and childlike within serious phases of my life. Thank you for seeing a strong woman and knowing that my power has no limits. Thank you for loving me, but most importantly, thank you for choosing me every single day. You have been an exhibitor of strength, healing, and perseverance within your own life, which has been the model for so much of my growth. I still remember the moment I first saw you and an inherent wish to be with you was formed. While we have been chasing one another since I was fourteen, there is one universal truth of my life: we were meant to be together in this lifetime. I love you deeply and endlessly.

Meet the Author

Scout Sobel is the founder of Scout's Agency and the co-host of the popular Okay Sis Podcast. She is a trailblazer in the media industry for utilizing podcasts as a powerful form of PR. After starting Okay Sis, which focuses on female guests, Scout fell in love with spreading women's stories and identified the rising popularity and influence of podcasting. She started Scout's Agency with an emphasis in podcast PR for women entrepreneurs, podcasters, and brands.

Within a year and a half of starting Scout's Agency, she had run podcast tours for high-profile women like Catt Sadler, Kelley Baker, and Rebecca Minkoff and booked major celebrities on her clients' podcasts as guests such as Brian Grazer, Colbie Caillat, Sophia Amoruso, and Jillian Michaels - all with no prior connections. She also landed brands like Bala and Kelley Baker Brows in publications like Marie Claire, Vogue, Harper's Bazaar, PEOPLE, WhoWhatWear, Essence, Forbes, amongst others.

Prior to her work on Okay Sis and Scout's Agency, Scout started her own magazine which was sold in Barnes & Noble and newsstands nationwide. Musician Halsey graced the cover of the third edition. Her magazine led to her being brought on as the Director of Operations to help launch the popular women's mentorship media site, Entitymag.com.

Scout's success did not come without trials and tribulations. She has been living with a severe case of bipolar disorder for 15 years. She was once unable to hold a job, go to college, or function in today's society. With a lot of self-development work, Scout manages her bipolar disorder successfully and uses her mental strength to fuel her entrepreneurial dreams. She uses her mental health journey to inspire other women to feel safe in their emotions and follow their entrepreneurial calling with her solo-podcast, SCOUT.

You can follow Scout on Instagram @scoutsobel and find out more at www.scoutsobel.com

Made in the USA
Las Vegas, NV
11 April 2022